heart & soul
CAREER
TUNE-UP

heart & soul

CAREER TUNE-UP

 **7 NEVER-BEFORE-PUBLISHED SECRETS TO CAPTURING HEART & SOUL IN YOUR WORK LIFE**

CHUCK COCHRAN
DONNA PEERCE

CERTIFIED PROFESSIONAL
RESUME WRITERS AND PARTNERS,
HEART & SOUL CAREER CENTER

DAVIES-BLACK PUBLISHING • PALO ALTO, CALIFORNIA

NOTICE

All names have been changed to protect the privacy of the individuals highlighted in this book. Any similarities to actual persons, living or dead, are purely coincidental.

Published by Davies-Black Publishing, an imprint of Consulting Psychologists Press, Inc., 3803 East Bayshore Road, Palo Alto, CA 94303; 800-624-1765; www.daviesblack.com

Special discounts on bulk quantities of Davies-Black books are available to corporations, professional associations, and other organizations. For details, contact the Director of Book Sales at Davies-Black Publishing, an imprint of Consulting Psychologists Press, Inc., 3803 East Bayshore Road, Palo Alto, CA 94303; 650-691-9123; Fax 650-623-9271.

Visit the Davies-Black Publishing web site at www.daviesblack.com.

Cover and interior design by Seventeenth Street Studios

04 03 02 01 00   10 9 8 7 6 5 4 3 2 1
Printed in the United States of America

Library of Congress Cataloging-in-Publication Data
Cochran, Chuck
    Heart & soul career tune-up : 7 never-before-published secrets to capturing heart & soul in your work life / Chuck Cochran, Donna Peerce.
      p.   cm.
    Includes bibliographical references and index.
    ISBN 0-89106-141-X (pbk)
    1. Career development—United States. I. Title: Heart and soul career tune-up.
    II. Peerce, Donna. III. Title.
    HF5381 .C66394 2000
    650.1—dc21

                                  99-086522

FIRST EDITION
First printing 2000

To my amazing wife, Michelle, and awesome son, Dean!

CHUCK COCHRAN

I would like to say thanks to my family, friends, Melinda Adams Merino,
God, my spiritual Master and the Dream Master for all the wonderful gifts in my life.

DONNA PEERCE

Contents

Preface

Hello, friend, and welcome. We are the *Heart & Soul* career authors—perhaps you've heard of us, or perhaps not. It doesn't matter. What does matter is that you have found this book, and because you've picked it up, we know we have something to offer you. As Heart & Soul career authors, we believe that all of life is a Heart & Soul experience and that your career is a Heart & Soul journey, too, just like any other part of your life.

Be assured that this is not your typical career book. It's not a quick fix to all your career problems, so if that's what you're looking for, then stop. If that's all you really want, then it's doubtful that you're going to be very successful in your career anyway—because there are no quick fixes for career problems, just as there are no quick fixes for our lives.

We believe it is important for you to get to the root of your problems in your career, because your career is more than likely a reflection of how your life is going. If you have problems in your career, it's probably because there are problems in your everyday life—issues that you haven't addressed and problems that you haven't mastered.

Temporary solutions won't work. You have to get to the heart and soul—the inner depths—of your problems and create permanent solutions to resolve those issues. This is the only way that your Heart & Soul career tune-up will be effective.

Everyone should be working on implementing Heart & Soul career tune-ups throughout their lives. If you're not doing this, you're cheating yourself. That's why this book is for you—especially if you are someone who wants more than just an ordinary job, an ordinary career, an ordinary life. You want to know and understand yourself—your drives, problems, weaknesses, and strengths. You want to live the life you will love—the life you were born to live. You want to pursue your mission in life—your higher purpose. You believe in the Heart & Soul way of living, of incorporating these principles into your everyday existence and your everyday job.

In this book, we offer you numerous Heart & Soul tools and techniques to help you manage your Heart & Soul career tune-up. This book offers real-life stories about individuals who have used these tools and successfully turned around their lives and careers. It gives you an opportunity to become better and enjoy life more! *Incorporating heart and soul into your career tune-up will make a real difference—we promise!*

Being happy in your career, as in life, is an up-and-down process. Some days are good and some days are bad. With the growth of the Internet and the ongoing trend of corporate downsizing, transferring, and rightsizing, you have to be flexible, adaptable, and prepared. Many people don't know how to handle the emotional roller coaster in today's career world—or in the world at all. All the new technology plus the ongoing problems in our evolving world has left many people off balance and wondering, "What can I do? What is wrong with my career—with my life? Why can't I find a good job? Why can't I be happy in my job? Why do I have to work with people I don't like or who don't agree with my work style? Am I destined to always work in a job I don't like? Do I need to upgrade my education and skills?" Are these some of your questions? If so, relax! We can help you!

Not many people find that perfect job, or that perfect life, right away. Not many know how to find happiness at all, but one thing is for sure: Your career is an integral part of your life and your happiness. If your career is not moving forward in alignment with yourself and your dreams, your life is probably off-kilter, and this can cause you all kinds of emotional and physical problems.

Being happy with your career and life, as well as managing the problems that come your way, is an ongoing process. It involves combining several proactive Heart & Soul tools, disciplines, and strategies. It involves knowing who you are, knowing your mission or higher purpose, and what your life is all about—why you're here on Earth, why you're the person you are, and what you can do in this world to make a difference. Too often, people just get by. They live in a perpetual fog and have no idea what life is all about and why they're here. We believe that you want to wake up—that you want to know why you're here and how you can be better. We believe that you want to be the best you can be.

This book incorporates a synergistic, holistic approach to helping you in your career and, ultimately, in your life. It will help you understand and know yourself. It will help you tune in to your inner self where life's messages and guidance are waiting. Whether tuning up your career means finding a new job, transferring within your company, learning to embrace others' diversity, upgrading your skills, finding a company that matches your own goals and dreams, confronting emotional problems that affect your career, learning how to be happy in your current position, or changing careers completely, this book will help you. *Heart & Soul Career Tune-Up* is for anyone who is serious about achieving, revamping, and tuning up his or her career, as well as acomplishing his or her career goals and dreams. It's about turning dreams into reality. It's a practical tool for preparing yourself for all the career challenges and stresses that life throws your way. It offers the "seven never-before-published secrets to capturing Heart & Soul in your work life." So, as you embrace the new century, you can be more confident, poised, happy, and successful.

We offer this book to you as a way to help you understand yourself, your life, and the problems you face in today's career world. We'll explore why you're having problems and how you can overcome even the most difficult challenges. We'll take you on an inner Heart & Soul journey that will help all your outer journeys be more successful.

Heart & Soul Career Tune-Up is our third book in the *Heart & Soul* career series. It is independent of our other two books, *Heart & Soul Resumes* and *Heart & Soul Internet Job Search*. All three books complement one another and can be used together or separately. Our books focus on an in-depth, psychological, "Heart & Soul" way of living. Whether you are dealing with your career or personal endeavors, our books will help you. If you embrace our principles and follow our suggestions, we are confident that you'll grow to become a better you—professionally, intellectually, mentally, physically, and spiritually.

So, join us, won't you? We invite you to join us in our third "Heart & Soul" career adventure. There's one thing we can promise—it will change your life!

—CHUCK COCHRAN AND DONNA PEERCE

Checking Your Alignment

You are today where your thoughts brought you...
You will be tomorrow
Where your thoughts take you.

JAMES ALLEN

ALIGNMENT, WITH REGARD TO your Heart & Soul career tune-up, allows you to capitalize on your strengths and the strengths of others. If your life and career path are not properly aligned, then chances are your career is bumpy, wobbly, and even veering off in the wrong direction. You don't want to waste time on the wrong career path!

You can align your career, ideals, and spirit to achieve a successful synergy. Whether you align with your current company, or you hope to align with a future employer, this holistic Heart & Soul synergy catapults you and your current or prospective employer to achieve fantastic results.

HEART & SOUL TIP

Your personal goals must align with your employer's in order for you both to be successful.

If you haven't achieved proper alignment in your career, you may feel complacent, undervalued, and even bored with your career and life. That is why aligning your career, ideals, and spirit with those of your employer is the first secret to capturing heart and soul in your work life.

CAREER
SUCCESS
STORY

Bob Sandusky

Always the center of attention at large family gatherings, Bob was the life of the party. Every year for 55 years—basically every year since Bob was born—his family had met for a huge reunion. Bob's father, now 76 years old, usually organized the meeting for a weekend around the 4th of July. Bob's immediate and extended family was large (about 150 people), but usually about 50 people showed up each year—Bob and about 20 other die-hard family members plus others.

Every year, as family members arrived throughout the morning, "Uncle Bob" would settle into position. He favored a comfortable chair that would stay in the shade throughout the day so he could hold court for anyone who'd listen. He'd begin telling stories as soon as the first child sat down beside him. With each story, more people would gather around to listen to Bob's tall tales.

Bob had a real knack for bringing people together and making them feel good about themselves. Bob's father knew this, and this was probably one of the main reasons he continued to organize these family events. He was proud of his son, and he and Bob were very close.

Back in Bob's hometown, Atlanta, 150 people worked at a furious pace at Judder Enterprises, a door manufacturer. The company had received an order for 1,000 doors, sold last week by Bob Sandusky, with a promised delivery date of just a few days away. Amid some company skepticism, Bob had convinced the manufacturer that it could deliver the order on time—the company could really use the revenue generated by such a large order.

Bob was known as a motivator at Judder. He was constantly challenged and truly loved his work. He was respected by the employees, trusted by the ownership, and admired by his boss. During his 20-some years with Judder, Bob was promoted to virtually every major management position, including sales, his favorite position with the company.

As the company grew, what had been a small and close-knit shop became more and more automated and bureaucratic. Bob's style was quite the opposite—he loved people and relationships. He despised the forms, paperwork, and administrative controls that were a part of the growing operation.

When Judder was sold to a major home-manufacturing conglomerate, the automated, corporate kinds of requirements became even more restrictive. A new corporate management team took over the once-small business, and

Bob felt more discouraged about the company and his job. The new management had distinctly different opinions than Bob about how to conduct business.

Bob, an awesome salesperson, had never positioned himself as the key to the client relationship. In fact, for the sake of the business, Bob wanted all of his clients to get to know and trust as many people in Judder as possible. That way, if he wasn't available, the clients would always have a contact at the company to help them. What this meant to Bob was that he was not absolutely vital in keeping the company's existing client base.

Unfortunately, that didn't work to Bob's advantage. When he unselfishly introduced other key people into his sales relationships, he unknowingly positioned himself for termination. His style of business and the new corporate managers' style of business clashed dramatically, and they let him go.

Bob had outgrown his job because he was no longer aligned with his employer. Although he could have conformed to the new management style, he wouldn't have been happy, and he knew it. It was time for him to move on. While he wasn't sure what the future held for him, he did know that his career needed a tune-up.

He enjoyed talking with people and made it a goal to have a job that involved working with people and sharing his experiences. He felt confident that life would present new career opportunities for him if he would just "go with the flow" and remain open and patient, which is exactly what happened.

At his most recent family reunion, Bob was in rare form. Everyone stayed in the shade and listened to Bob. He had a unique way of reaching everyone. Tears were streaming down the faces of kids and adults alike, they were laughing so hard.

Bob told us that during a break from the fun, his brother-in-law invited him to speak at his company's annual meeting. At first Bob dismissed the idea, but his brother-in-law persisted, so Bob decided to give it a go. He thought that perhaps this speaking engagement would turn out to be something valuable. And it was.

Eight months later, after Bob's speech at a Florida hotel, 250 people gave the longest standing ovation in the company's history. They loved him! And Bob loved speaking to them! He hadn't felt this exhilarated in a long, long time! This was just what his career needed! A new twist! A new adventure! Bob's public-speaking career had begun with a jump-start!

Meeting organizers quickly responded to the buzz about this new speaker on the circuit and started booking engagements featuring Bob at $5,000 a pop. Within a few months, Bob's calendar for the following year was completely full! Bob told us he had never thought he would love any work more than the early days at Judder, but his new public-speaking career took the cake. It was in perfect alignment with his love for talking with people and sharing his years of expertise and knowledge. Bob experienced a new zest for living—all as a result of "going with the flow" and tuning up his career to match his goals.

Bob started his career in full alignment with Judder, grew out of alignment with the "new" Judder and new management philosophies, and came around in perfect alignment with his new speaking career. Once in alignment with his new speaking career, Bob was implementing a true Heart & Soul approach to life and his career.

Meeting Obligations

HEART & SOUL TIP

You have an obligation to yourself and to your employer to align yourself with the goals of the company, change the company, or leave.

To achieve a successful career, you have an obligation to yourself and to your employer to align yourself with the goals of the company, try to change the company, or leave. Sometimes, changing the company will not be possible, so you'll face either changing your attitude or leaving.

Your employer should be obliged to create a culture that is welcoming and appealing to the employees, but that doesn't always happen. If a company is not satisfied with its performance or with the performance of its employees, it has two options: change the company or accept and manage high employee turnover. Many businesses can't survive a high turnover rate. If they are to survive, many employers are forced to dig deep down and make difficult changes to their operations and culture.

Finding Common Ground

In any relationship, the basis for alignment and mutual respect is finding common ground. Your special skills and strengths are different from anyone else's, but you also have values and principles in common with others. A good way to explore this issue is to analyze leadership styles you like and dislike—because we all know what it's like to have a boss you like and one you don't!

HEART & SOUL TIP

Your employer is obligated to define and follow a consistent business strategy and recruit accordingly, and you are obligated to research and understand what your employer will expect of you throughout your employment. Whether you work for two months or 20 years, you need to know what is expected of you.

Use Worksheet 1.1 to list what you have liked and disliked about any of your previous bosses. In other words, what do you think is representative of a good boss and a bad boss?

We borrowed an idea from popular speaker Richard Daft, author of *Fusion Leadership,* who often polls the attendees of his workshops on the various aspects of leadership. We polled a random sample of our clients and asked them to complete the exercise in Worksheet 1.1, listing examples and characteristics of good and bad bosses. Our survey included a variety of employees—from production line workers to senior managers.

GOOD BOSS

BAD BOSS

■ **WORKSHEET 1.1**
Describe a "Good" Boss and a "Bad" Boss

Bad Boss	Good Boss
Selfish	Has integrity
Disrespectful	Fair
Condescending	Honest
Deceitful	Moral
Makes false promises	Trusting
Poor communicator	Excellent communicator
Micromanager	Motivator
Behaves irrationally	Consistent
Not accountable	Defines responsibilities
Lazy	Enthusiastic

■ **TABLE 1.1**
How the Group Described "Good" and "Bad" Leadership

You might expect that the senior managers would have an entirely different view from the support personnel—that each tier of management would bring its own spin on effective leadership style. However, what we experienced was exactly the opposite. Every person we polled came up with basically the same ideas (see Table 1.1)

Good leadership has nothing to do with a person's position within the management hierarchy. Instead, good leadership comes from fundamentally sound and universally appreciated Heart & Soul principles and practices. Valuing diversity (which we discuss in Chapter 2) allows you and your manager to appreciate and understand people's differences, but it takes an appreciation and understanding of the areas in which you are alike to be a good leader.

Many a would-be leader's style reflects the leadership style that is influencing him or her. That is, your idea of good leadership is the same as that of your boss and your boss's boss. Unfortunately, if the culture of the company or the leadership style of the top brass is ineffective, poor leadership will permeate the entire organization.

Part of your Heart & Soul career tune-up is to understand what you want out of your company in terms of leadership and culture. You can't just take a new job or stay at a current job because it pays well and it has decent benefits. Instead, you need to thoroughly study and analyze who you are working for or who you are considering working for to implement a true Heart & Soul approach in your career tune-up and to align yourself with the right company or career.

HEART & SOUL TIP

Good leadership has nothing to do with one's level in the management hierarchy. It comes from fundamentally sound and universally appreciated Heart & Soul principles and practices.

Finding a Heart & Soul Company

Every organization possesses its own personality. By melding together the interests, values, and personalities of all the participants in an organization, a company defines its own culture. The leaders and the founders have the most input regarding the organization's culture, but every person, no matter how new or inexperienced, also contributes to the organization's culture. Your Heart & Soul employer's culture should align closely with your own.

HEART & SOUL TIP

Every person, no matter how new or inexperienced, contributes to the organization's culture. Find an employer whose culture aligns closely with your own.

Heart & Soul companies employ people who support the company's culture and mission. Everyone's vision should align with that of other employees and with the company's. Some companies employ people who are not all in tune with the organization's mission. As a result, the company lacks a unified force.

A Heart & Soul company and its employees have a profound understanding of who they are and what sort of people they are or want to be. After a few conversations with a business's employees, you can usually tell whether they work for a Heart & Soul company. If you feel energized and excited after meeting only a few people, and you can express what the company stands for and how dedicated its employees are to reaching their goals, you'll know you've located a true Heart & Soul company. Heart & Soul companies, whether they be big multinational firms or small two-person shops, educate and lead their employees first and then empower their workers to make decisions autonomously.

So how can you align yourself with a Heart & Soul company? The answer depends on your needs and the type of company you work for. You may not need to go looking for a new employer; instead you may want to become the new star in your own company! You can become the change agent in your organization that turns the company into one with heart and soul. You can use your own positive attitude and optimistic outlook on life to effectively make changes at work. Often, it just takes one person to effect a dramatic change within an organization.

You may be able to assume that your company's leaders want their company to be a Heart & Soul company, but they just don't know it yet. Or they may not relate to the Heart & Soul concept or terminology. But you can use a few of these phrases to get their attention and win them over to the Heart & Soul approach:

- Dramatically reduce employee turnover
- Create productive, working relationships among cross-functional teams
- Increase the company's profit margins
- Reduce internal conflict
- Improve customer relations
- Realize a loyal clientele with increased retention rates, repeat business, and referrals

- Retain employees who take pride and ownership in their work
- Increase quality and productivity
- Improve worker attitude
- Create an enjoyable work environment

If you want more information on turning your company into one with heart and soul, contact our office or e-mail us at heartsoul@mindspring.com.

If you decide that you need to change jobs, you can find Heart & Soul companies and market your skills to them. This may sound simple, but getting to know a company on an intimate level takes time. The only way to fully understand the culture of a company is to do business with it or talk to people who work there. Small and medium-sized privately held companies are difficult to research, yet they often hold the greatest opportunity for growth. These are the companies that you want to target!

Using KSAs: Knowledge, Skills, and Abilities

To achieve career alignment, you must first determine what knowledge, skills, and abilities (KSAs) your employer expects from someone in your position or in a position you're considering. In short, KSAs are the practical skills and education that are required to complete a particular job. For example, a college professor's KSAs would be a Ph.D. degree, teaching experience, and recent published work. A graphic designer would need specific skills in desktop publishing programs, experience designing for commercial projects, and other design-related KSAs.

Knowing your KSAs and those needed for your job will help you lay the foundation for your career alignment. Following are Worksheets 1.2 and 1.3, two KSA exercises. The first asks you to list the KSAs that are required for your current position or for one you are considering. The second exercise asks you to list your own personal KSAs. Try to come up with as many KSAs as you can for a particular job—think 10 to 50. Imagine that you are about to hire someone to fill your position. Ask yourself, "What are the basic requirements needed of each qualified applicant?" This might help you organize your thoughts.

Compare your KSAs with those needed to do your current job. Are you underutilized? Do you have great talents and skills that are not being fully used? Rarely does any one job fully utilize all of your KSAs; however, if you have defined certain skills that you want to use and practice but you cannot use them in your current position, consider this a big red flag: You may be out of alignment.

Try to restructure your job by adding new responsibilities and ridding yourself of others so that you use the KSAs that are of most interest to you. Position yourself and your career so you can be challenged at every level of your capacity. Does this repositioned job resemble your current job, or does it look like a different job entirely?

HEART & SOUL TIP

Position yourself and your career so you can be challenged at every level of your capacity.

CURRENT JOB KSAs

List the KSAs that are required to do your job. Put an asterisk by the KSAs you acquired while with your current employer. Use another sheet if you need more room.

■ **WORKSHEET 1.2**
Define the KSAs of Your Current Job (or One You're Considering)

SELF-DEFINED KSAs

List your KSAs in the space below. Put an asterisk by those that are underutilized or not used at all by your current employer. Use another sheet if you need more room.

■ **WORKSHEET 1.3**
Define Your Own KSAs

Strategic Goals

Develop, by reading your company's literature or by conducting your own research, the strategic goals of your company. (Don't just say "profit!" That's too easy and too obvious.) Ask yourself by what means your employer or prospective employer will earn its profitability or market share. Consider the exercise in Worksheet 1.4 on pages 12 and 13 to help you develop your thoughts.

SWOT Analysis

HEART & SOUL TIP

Look at the business from the owner's perspective. If you owned the business, what would you do with it? Try to gain a clear perspective for an employer's behavior.

"SWOT" stands for strengths, weaknesses, opportunities, and threats. Strengths and weaknesses concern internal operations—policies, employees, and plans. Opportunities and threats concern the external environment—competition, ventures, and outside influences. If you can identify and understand your company's SWOT, you can better determine your alignment with the company. Without going into too much detail, consider a SWOT analysis for your company (or department). Your alignment may become more and more clear when you start looking at the company from the stockholders' perspective. See Worksheet 1.5 on page 14.

Now that you have analyzed your company, it's time to think about the good stuff—you! Work through the following exercises (Worksheets 1.6 through 1.8 on pages 15 through 17) to help identify and explore your life objectives. You will compare and contrast your goals with your company's goals to check for proper Heart & Soul alignment.

HEART & SOUL TIP

You shouldn't have to wait forever to make only tiny incremental steps toward your dreams.

These are all important questions, so don't jump to conclusions. Certainly you can't expect your job to quickly afford you everything you've ever wanted, but at the same time you shouldn't have to wait forever to realize your goals.

Company Culture Versus Your Values

How well your company's culture fits with your values can make a dramatic difference in how well you're aligned with your job and employer. For example, how are people expected to behave in your organization? Compare this with how you personally would like them to behave. What differences do you see? What is important to you? What are your values and what sort of employer do you want to be associated with?

Use Worksheet 1.9 on page 18 to compare your company's culture with your own personal values.

Describe the Company's Suppliers and Target Customers

Detail the company's suppliers and customers. What is important to your company with regard to these issues? How will these criteria shape the future of your company? Although there are no right or wrong answers, you should think through these questions carefully.

Describe the Company's Sales and Marketing Plan

Detail everything you can about the company's sales and marketing strategy. What is important to your company with regard to these issues? How will these criteria shape the future of your company?

■ **WORKSHEET 1.4**
Describe Your Company

Describe the Company's Operational and Administrative Plan

Detail everything you can about the company's operational and administrative strategy. What is important to your company with regard to these issues? How will these criteria shape the future of your company?

Describe the Company's Staffing and Human Resources Plan

Detail everything you can about the company's staffing and human resources strategy. What is important to your company with regard to these issues? How will these criteria shape the future of your company? What sorts of people is your company looking for? What sort of environment does the company provide for employees? What does it expect from its employees?

Strengths (Internal)
List the company's strengths.

Weaknesses
List the company's weaknesses.

Opportunities
List the opportunities that the company could exploit.

Threats
List the threats that could damage your company.

■ **WORKSHEET 1.5**
Analyze Your Company's SWOT

List the top 10 to 20 most important things you would like to accomplish in your lifetime.

All of our books discuss living with a mission and goal setting, both of which are important to your alignment. A fun and easy way to explore your goals is to simply decide what you want to accomplish in your lifetime. The power of this Heart & Soul exercise is in its simplicity. Think long and hard about these goals.

1.

2.

3.

4.

5.

6.

7.

8.

9.

10.

11.

12.

13.

14.

15.

16.

17.

18.

19.

20.

■ **WORKSHEET 1.6**
List Your Desired Accomplishments

Write out the life goals you must develop to achieve the accomplishments you listed in Worksheet 1.6.

■ **WORKSHEET 1.7**
List Your Life Goals

Based on your current situation, your current career path, your KSAs, the KSAs required in your job, your goals, and your company's business strategy, which of your top 25 accomplishments will you achieve if you

Stay on the same career path?

Stay in the same job?

Stay with the same company?

Based on what you want to accomplish, your KSAs, your dreams, and everything you stand for, is your current position—or any position you are considering—helping or hindering you in meeting your life's objectives?

■ **WORKSHEET 1.8**
Explore the Necessary KSAs for Your Job, Goals, and Strategy

Your Company Culture	Your Personal Values

Describe similarities and how you are closely aligned with your company.

Describe differences and how you are not aligned.

■ **WORKSHEET 1.9**
  Compare Your Company's Culture and Your Personal Values

The goal of this chapter is to emphasize the importance of proper alignment and to provide you with some Heart & Soul tools to help you check and adjust your alignment. If these exercises illustrated more personal differences with your employer than you expected, that may be fine. Don't make any hasty decisions about your future just yet. Rash decisions based on raw emotion usually hurt all parties involved. If you identify a large gap in alignment, remember, as we mentioned earlier, that you have a few options: You can keep the status quo, you can change the company, you can reposition yourself with the company to take advantage of a better alignment, or you can plan to leave the company and begin a career change or job search.

HEART & SOUL TIP

You may align perfectly with an employer for your entire career, or you may align well with a company for only a few years or less. People outgrow companies just as they outgrow fads and trends.

Before you decide to change anything, we recommend that you discuss your options with as many decision makers as possible. Talk though the issues that you've identified in these exercises. Make your life decisions based on sound reason and logical analysis. Do whatever it takes to put yourself in a position where you will be in perfect alignment with your employer.

These are your life and your dreams—so take your time in the planning and developmental stages of your ideas. Taking time to consider your Heart & Soul career tune-up will greatly benefit you as you journey through your life and career. Remember, the time you spend up front will serve you well in the long run!

CAREER SUCCESS STORY

The Kingston Company

The Kingston Company was a small, $20-million company that sold "widgets" around the world. It employed 50 people—10 sales reps, 25 manufacturing people, 10 support personnel, and 5 senior managers. The company had been in business for more than 20 years and had grown steadily over the years from a small, family-run business.

In time, Kingston needed to compete with the major international "players" to keep growing. The culture that permeated the organization was one of loyalty and a relaxed hometown family feeling. Kingston had always been a Heart & Soul company and had always adopted policies that encouraged training, longevity, generous retirement benefits, and the like.

Kingston hired a consultant to help it determine how to compete with the big guys. The consultant told the company it needed to set up an aggressive sales incentive program. Sales reps would have to meet strict quotas or be fired. The consultant said the only way to grow was to take on a cold, hard-nosed approach to sales and the acquisition of new business.

Kingston had built its reputation and previous success on an entirely different mentality, however. The company had always encouraged its sales reps not to sell based on quotas. It encouraged sales staff to educate and assist clientele and to sell only what was in a client's best interest. Kingston believed that if sales reps built lasting, long-term, and trusting relationships with customers, the business would continue and grow. Eventually, customers would learn that Kingston treated its customers right by never gouging them or profiting unnecessarily. To encourage this culture among sales reps, Kingston used a compensation plan somewhat unique in the industry: It paid sales reps a straight salary with no commission.

Even with ups and downs, and unusual sales tactics, 20 years later the company had a huge database of active, loyal, and pleased customers. But Kingston desperately wanted to grow, so management took the consultant's advice and set up strict sales quotas and a straight commission incentive plan.

HEART & SOUL TIP

Employers may attract and encourage long-term employees, short-term employees, peak performers, low-wage employees, or highly skilled people. Identify your employer's business strategy and employment package and see how well your goals align with those of your employer.

We offer this story only as a basis for discussion and realize that this particular case may be dependent on factors we have not presented here. However, based on the information above, can you determine whether Kingston was aligned with its goals and its employees? Would Kingston be aligned with the culture of the company if it were to adopt a dramatically different compensation plan?

As you might imagine, the sales reps were appalled and insulted at the new straight commission plan, and the tension was thick after the new plan took effect. Kingston went from a small, well-aligned, low-turnover, and highly profitable manufacturing company to a struggling, cutthroat, cynical, and untrusting organization. After six months of the new commission system, the damage was done. The sales force returned to the old salary format, but only after 15 of Kingston's best people left the job. Kingston is on a slow recovery path and has learned a great lesson in the process.

The Kingston Company had originally hired a certain kind of sales rep that enjoyed building long-term relationships and earning a straight salary, but the consultant wanted Kingston to hire competitive, hard-driving, commissioned sales reps. One could make a case for both theories, but Kingston had set a precedent, or established a company culture, 20 years earlier. The consultant's recommendations were in conflict with the company's culture, and the results of the changes were disastrous.

HEART & SOUL TIP

Employers and their employees must align their values, goals, and principles if they want the relationship to be a successful one!

In any career situation, what matters most is that you are in alignment with your job, with your career—that your ethics, career goals, and mission in life match those of your company. If these don't match, you know that your career is out of alignment and needs adjusting. Proper alignment is a vital facet of your overall Heart & Soul career tune-up.

2 Embracing Diversity

To know others is wisdom;
To know oneself is enlightenment.

TAO TE CHING

A S INFANTS, WE FEEL anxious when a strange person picks us up; as toddlers we learn that the hot stove top burns when we touch it. Impression after impression, we learn what brings us pleasure and what brings us pain.

Throughout our lives, we receive stimuli that make impressions on us. These impressions, positive and negative, form our reality. In our formative years, a single stimulus can make a dramatic change in how we view the world. Later in life, however, bumping up against the cumulative effect of millions of impressions, new stimuli can make only incremental differences in our reality. This is how each person's individual "world," or reality, is formed—a combination of stimuli and the impressions they make. Each person's reality is as unique as a snowflake—we're all similar, but no two of us are exactly alike.

HEART & SOUL TIP

Our perception of reality is a reflection of our experiences since birth. While we may share an experience or situation with others, we each interpret it in our own unique way.

HEART & SOUL TIP

By understanding and valuing our differences, our career goals and ambitions take on greater meaning.

HEART & SOUL TIP

By embracing others' differences, and by aligning your goals, ideals, and spirit with those of your co-workers, customers, bosses, and suppliers, you can do almost anything!

Each being has something wonderful to contribute to life, based on his or her experiences and on the ways those experiences have been interpreted. Understanding and learning to embrace and value diversity is our second never-before-published secret to capturing heart and soul in your work life.

One of your first lessons in life is that your reality is merely your own perception based on your experiences and unique interpretations. Perception and reality, in large part, are the basis for many of our differences in opinions, outlook, and lifestyle. In this chapter we want to explore human behavior and how we can benefit personally and professionally when we open our minds and our hearts to the diverse world around us. By understanding and valuing people's differences, our career goals and ambitions can take on much more meaning.

As you explore new careers or try to invigorate your existing career, think about the ways in which you interact with other people. How do you fit in this world? What can you do to fulfill your goals? What kinds of people do you enjoy working with? What strengths to you bring to the table, and what strengths do you seek from others? What are your weaknesses and what are some potential pitfalls in how you build and maintain relationships in the workplace? These are all very important questions, and you must quantify your answers to get the most out of your Heart & Soul career tune-up!

Individually, our efforts may result in only limited success, but united with others, we can reach even higher goals. By embracing and valuing others' differences, and by aligning your goals, ideals, and spirit with those of your co-workers, customers, bosses, and suppliers, you can move mountains!

Drawing Strength from the Diversity Around You

By valuing and embracing diversity, you have an opportunity to explore, appreciate, and benefit from the different strengths each of us has to offer. Consciously or not, fairly or unfairly, we judge people. Unfairly, we can prejudge (or have prejudice against) people based on looks, stereotypes, or circumstances. Fairly, we can judge people with the open and honest knowledge of our own shortcomings. Fair judgment is not about criticism; it is about "understanding." When we can capture and embrace our own weaknesses and strengths and learn to value the differences in others, we can accomplish so much more then we ever imagined—in both our personal and professional lives.

As you learn about appreciating diversity and aligning your goals with those of your company, you must also recognize and understand factors about yourself that contribute to your success or failure in your career and life. Knowing yourself will help you understand how you react to others and how they react to you.

It is essential that you recognize and understand your true Heart & Soul self, whether you're trying to make new friends in a new work environment or trying to change yourself or your company. Remember, all of our strategies work together in a synergistic, holistic pattern to create a true Heart & Soul approach to tuning up your self, your career, and your life. It is only when these components are working together that you will experience your greatest growth and accomplishments.

HEART & SOUL TIP

When we can accept our weaknesses and our strengths, and understand and value the differences in others, we can accomplish so much more!

Finding Diversity Outside Your Clique

One of the first things you do when you start a new job or program to make yourself feel like you belong is make friends. From your first day on the job, you get to know a lot of people and start to connect with a handful of others. Particularly in large group settings, cliques can start to form. You enjoy the allies you have created and begin to feel more comfortable and confident in your job as your friendships develop. You can complain about your job or discuss how changes could be made. You can help one another in dealing with the internal politics of the organization. You can even socialize after work.

Developing cliques is normal and healthy, but you can benefit by taking the initiative to get to know people outside your clique. Try stepping out of your comfort zone and meeting new people. You may find that you get to know and appreciate a new and different person who could someday be a close friend or confidante. Don't leave your old friends or colleagues behind, but continually add more and more people to your "A list." Your life will be richer with each new person you meet.

HEART & SOUL TIP

Reach out to people you don't know. Expand your mind. Break out of the clique and appreciate and value the diversity that is around you right now!

Based on the people who are a part of your world right now, use Worksheet 2.1 on pages 24 and 25 to help identify how these people fit into your various spheres of influence.

List people in your closest sphere of influence (family and close friends).

List people in your next sphere of influence (friends).

List people in your next sphere of influence (influential acquaintances).

■ **WORKSHEET 2.1**
Explore Your Sphere of Influence

List people in your next sphere of influence (acquaintances).

List people in your next sphere of influence (don't know personally).

List people in your next sphere of influence (don't know, but work together).

■ **WORKSHEET 2.1 CONTINUED**
Explore Your Sphere of Influence

Use these lists to help identify people you would like to get to know better. Challenge yourself to forge new relationships. You will be glad you did!

Joshua Taylor

When Joshua Taylor was hired as the creative director for an international advertising agency in Chicago, the company vice president told him, "We've been having a difficult time with our creative staff. They are all very talented individuals, but they have trouble working together, and as a result, jobs aren't getting completed on time and we're losing clients."

When Joshua asked, "What seems to be the problem?" the vice president replied, "We don't KNOW what the problem is. Our last creative director simply couldn't motivate the staff even though he tried. We're counting on you to turn things around."

Joshua had been a successful motivator in the past. He asked his new boss for a couple of weeks to get to know everyone. "I'll come up with a report on what I've observed and an assessment of the situation."

"Sure," the vice president said. "And if you think there are people we need to replace, then by all means, go ahead. The thing we need is a bunch of lazy folks who aren't producing."

Joshua was already feeling overwhelmed. This agency had been in trouble for a year or so and had lost several major accounts simply because the 20 members of the creative staff weren't producing as they should.

At his last job as creative director for a midsized advertising agency, he had been successful at resolving lots of problems. He had worked closely with and nurtured the creative team's 12 staff members. As a result, the small staff had won several prestigious advertising awards. But, he wondered, could he do as well here?

Joshua noticed that, even though the department had an entire floor to itself, the creative staff was bunched together in a maze of tiny cubicles. Conversations in one cubicle flooded into all the others, making it nearly impossible to concentrate. The graphic designer artists were lined up in a row, all facing the cublicles, and from what Joshua observed, they mostly laughed and talked among themselves instead of working.

He noticed one young woman, a copywriter, who sat at her keyboard in her cubicle and seemed to be in a world of her own. "Good morning," Joshua said as he approached her.

"Uh, . . . oh," she looked up sleepily, "hello."

"Did I disturb you?" he asked.

"No, I was just thinking," she said.

It was obvious she had been sleeping.

"I'm Joshua Taylor, the new creative director," he said, holding out his hand.

"Yes, I know," she said. "My name is Danielle Parsons."

"Written anything interesting lately?"

HEART & SOUL TIP

A good leader will learn about his or her staff members individual strengths and weaknesses and motivate them through nurturing and embracing diversity.

"No, not really."

"Well, is was good to meet you, and I'm sure we'll talk later," Joshua said, as he moved into the other cubicles. It was clear to him that Danielle was not a morning person and probably did her best work at night. Yet the offices opened at 8:00 A.M. each day and closed at 5:00 P.M.—not exactly great hours for a "night person."

Throughout his department, Joshua made notes about his staff. It was up to him to turn this department around, to make it productive and award winning, like his previous staff had been. He knew he had his job cut out for him. No one seemed to really care about his or her job, and motivation simply was not there.

He learned from his assistant that the former creative director had ruled with an iron fist. People were required to be at their desks exactly at 8 A.M. and lunch was precisely from noon to 1 P.M. every day. Joshua knew instinctively what the problem was: The creative department was like a prison that was

closely monitored by the warden. From his years of experience, he knew that creative people needed space and freedom to express themselves. He also knew that if he could help identify a worker's needs and strengths and nurture the strengths, he could help that worker achieve fantastic results. He had learned that it was important to embrace diversity in others and capitalize on it.

Joshua set up a meeting with his creative staff, creating a relaxed, inviting atmosphere by offering fruit, pastries, and coffee. He explained that he wanted to get to know each person and that he believed they were a talented group that needed freedom to perform in an environment that best served their needs. By the end of the meeting, Joshua had set up private meetings with each staff member.

He discovered that some workers preferred to have their own space. Several of the copywriters wanted private offices so that they could concentrate. He also knew that cubicles don't work for everyone, so he had some offices built. He also allowed workers to arrive at and leave the office at hours that accommodated their creative times—not at hours that were unreasonable for them.

Joshua investigated his staff thoroughly and discovered their interests, work habits, likes, and dislikes. They were a diverse group. He knew it was important to listen to their ideas, share their ideas with others, and embrace their differences. Thus, he turned his department around and became known as a "miracle worker."

As a result, his staff won several Addy Awards for outstanding work, and the agency grew in size and volume due to new accounts and repeat business. With expert leadership and guidance, Joshua had steered his group to the top.

Joshua knew how to recognize people's strengths and capitalize on them. He knew that people perform better when they have freedom and are allowed to work in an environment that's best suited to them. Whether you're a leader or just one of the team members in your company, you can learn to appreciate others' differences, too.

That's what embracing diversity is all about. It's about recognizing and understanding one another's differences and samenesses, respecting other people's choices and philosophies, and joining diverse philosophies and work habits together to create a Heart & Soul synergy that's always successful and productive. In any Heart & Soul career tune-up, its important that you recognize, accept, and embrace diversity. You can learn from it. Our world is an exciting place that is full of adventures, and if you view others with a sense of wonder and curiosity, you will soon understand just how much you can learn from those who aren't like you.

Worksheet 2.2, on pages 29 through 31, presents a creative visualization exercise that will make you think about others' differences. On each page is a statement about a potential co-worker that describes an aspect of this person's personality, culture, or work habits. As you work through the exercise, imagine how you will react to this individual—how you will nurture and embrace his or her diversity—and visualize the outcome. Read each description and write your responses in the space provided. Take time and put some thought into this creative visualization exercise.

Understanding Behavior

After you develop the Heart & Soul tools that help you tune up your life and accept who you are, you are better equipped to understand and accept the complexities of others. Naturally, when you understand your own inner heart and soul, you can better accept and embrace the diversity of others. Now it's time to learn how to implement your working style with others in a more direct and psychological way.

HEART & SOUL TIP

When you understand yourself and your own behavior, you can define a career path that fits you perfectly. When you understand the behavior of those around you, you can appreciate their strengths and be sensitive to their differences.

First we need to create a solid model of behavior and interaction so we can determine why some people work well together and some don't. We also need to explore why certain careers work well for some people and not others. As you develop the path for your career, you need to value and understand your behavior as well as that of others who work with you.

CREATIVE VISUALIZATION EXERCISE

Sabrina Matthews is a lovely young woman who tends to shy away from groups. She prefers one-on-one conversations or being alone in her office. She doesn't join the office group after work at the local bar. She often feels like she doesn't fit in and this sometimes affects her work. Imagine Sabrina in your work environment. What special talents or skills does she have that you can embrace? What would you do to make her feel welcome, appreciated, and nurtured? What can you learn from her?

■ **WORKSHEET 2.2**
Visualize Embracing Diversity

CREATIVE VISUALIZATION EXERCISE

Jacqueline Nichols is a top-rated psychotherapist. She's one of the best in her field, yet she is often criticized for not joining the other staff members in her office at lunchtime. Instead, she likes to use the time to organize the charts in her files. She not only stays thin by not eating lunch but is always ahead of the others in her administrative functions. Imagine how you would react to Jacqueline's methods of working. What can you learn from her?

■ **WORKSHEET 2.2 CONTINUED**
Visualize Embracing Diversity

CREATIVE VISUALIZATION EXERCISE

James Norton is an organizer and likes to serve on committees within the company. He's not afraid to speak up at meetings, and he's outspoken and often blunt in his opinions. Sometimes he hurts people's feelings with his honesty, but overall he's chatty, friendly, and thoughtful, and he works hard and does a good job. Imagine how you would react to James's methods of working. How would you respond to his honest, outspoken style? What can you learn from him?

■ **WORKSHEET 2.2 CONTINUED**
Visualize Embracing Diversity

Using Psychological Type

Swiss psychiatrist Carl Jung originally developed the theory of psychological type. This theory was further developed into practical applications by the mother-daughter team of Katharine Briggs and Isabel Myers, who developed the *Myers-Briggs Type Indicator®* (MBTI®) instrument. The MBTI instrument is an excellent tool we use to help our clients understand their behavior and strengths and determine what they need from their colleagues and employers.

We have included a broad overview of the MBTI instrument in the Appendix so you can approximate what your type is. Call your local career counselor or contact our office via e-mail at heartsoul@mindspring.com if you would like to take the MBTI instrument and receive a complete report, analysis, and professional interpretation. To use this book, the information in the Appendix should suffice.

HEART & SOUL TIP

Understanding and appreciating the differences between yourself and others will benefit you at a personal and a professional level.

The use of psychological type is particularly beneficial in valuing diversity for two reasons: (1) Determining your type will help you further analyze and consider career paths and job categories. It will allow you to reaffirm your commitment to your current career path or help you target other professional positions that might be more appropriate for you, given the circumstances in your life now. (2) Also, knowing your type will help you understand how to work more effectively with your colleagues. Understanding and appreciating the differences between you and others can help you realize success on a personal and a professional level.

We have included a few type exercises in Worksheet 2.3. If you have taken the MBTI instrument and you know your type, you can skip the exercises. If you have not taken the MBTI instrument, we recommend reading the Appendix now to estimate your most likely type. This will help you understand and benefit from the exercises on the next four pages.

Finding Trends in Your Behavior

Look back at your worksheets to find trends in how you act and react with certain kinds of people. Are you treating others differently than you expect to be treated? Think about relationships that are strained; can you attribute this to different personality types?

What a boring place this world would be if we were all the same. Diversity makes it dynamic. Instead of harboring fear and loathing for people who are different from you, you can value them for their strengths and differences. Recognize who you are and how you prefer to interact with others. Many times the things you dislike in others is just a reflection of what you don't like in yourself!

EXTRAVERSION–INTROVERSION

Based on the Extraversion–Introversion dichotomy, list the appropriate person in the first column and indicate whether you are more extraverted or introverted in your particular relationship with that person. Mark "E" for Extraversion and "I" for Introversion.

Then, in the third column, list whether the other person is more extraverted or introverted. For example, if you tend to stay quiet and pensive when you are with an in-law, you might mark "I" in the second column. If your in-law acts similarly, then you might mark "I" for him or her, too. Look for trends in how you act and react around others. Note whether the relationship is one in which you are the authority (you are the boss) or one in which you are the subordinate (the other is the boss).

Try to get a feeling for how you respond to different people in different settings.

Name	Do You Use "E" or "I"?	Does He/She Use "E" or "I"?
Spouse/Significant other:		
Child:		
In-law:		
Co-worker:		
Distant co-worker:		
Boss:		
Close friend:		
Acquaintance:		
Someone you just met:		
Direct report/Employee:		

■ **WORKSHEET 2.3**
Approximate Your Type

SENSING–INTUITION

Complete this form based on the Sensing–Intuition dichotomy. You may need to refer to the Appendix for further clarification. Mark "S" for Sensing and "N" for Intuition.

Name	Do You Use "S" or "N"?	Does He/She Use "S" or "N"?
Spouse/Significant other:		
Child:		
In-law:		
Co-worker:		
Distant co-worker:		
Boss:		
Close friend:		
Acquaintance:		
Someone you just met:		
Direct report/Employee:		

■ **WORKSHEET 2.3 CONTINUED**
Approximate Your Type

THINKING–FEELING

Complete this form based on the Thinking–Feeling dichotomy. You may need to refer to the Appendix for further clarification. Mark "T" for Thinking and "F" for Feeling.

Name	Do You Use "T" or "F"?	Does He/She Use "T" or "F"?
Spouse/Significant other:		
Child:		
In-law:		
Co-worker:		
Distant co-worker:		
Boss:		
Close friend:		
Acquaintance:		
Someone you just met:		
Direct report/Employee:		

■ **WORKSHEET 2.3 CONTINUED**
Approximate Your Type

JUDGING–PERCEIVING

Complete this form based on the Judging–Perceiving dichotomy. You may need to refer to the Appendix for further clarification. Mark "J" for Judging and "P" for Perceiving.

Name	Do You Use "J" or "P"?	Does He/She Use "J" or "P"?
Spouse/Significant other:		
Child:		
In-law:		
Co-worker:		
Distant co-worker:		
Boss:		
Close friend:		
Acquaintance:		
Someone you just met:		
Direct report/Employee:		

■ **WORKSHEET 2.3 CONTINUED**
Approximate Your Type

Above all, remember that if you truly know and understand the heart and soul of your being, then you will be more open to those who are different from you. This is absolutely crucial in any work environment. By being in tune with yourself, with life, you will be more successful in your career and better able to work with others who are unique and different. If you find that you are slipping backwards into a negative thought pattern concerning others, then practice those meditation exercises. Refocus.

Embrace diversity. Enjoy it! Each of us has specific talents and gifts to offer. Accept yours and those of others. By incorporating all these synergistic Heart & Soul ideas and exercises in your life and career, you will succeed and achieve your dreams and career goals—far faster than you ever imagined.

HEART & SOUL TIP

Embrace diversity. Enjoy it! Each of us has specific talents and gifts to offer. Accept yours and those of others.

Managing the Terrible Ten

*We make a living by what we get,
but we make a life by what we give.*

NORMAN MacEWAN

INSTEAD OF OFFERING ADVICE on what to do, as we have in our other books, we thought we would take a unique approach in this chapter and advise you what *not* to do! Avoiding the Terrible Ten career derailers is our third never-before-published secret to capturing heart and soul in your work life. These are the 10 worst mistakes any professional can make. An important part of your Heart & Soul career tune-up will be to brush up on the skills you need to avoid making these 10 mistakes.

Some of the issues we discuss are related to job search techniques, but they also apply to your career in general because they remind you that you should constantly be working on your professional goals. A strong career path is not

HEART & SOUL TIP

Formulate a life mission as well as a career goal.

one of steps and plateaus, but one that is constantly rising toward your highest goal. You should always be positioning yourself for a better job or career. In addition, having a mission is as important as always having a professional and current resume. What good is a career goal if you can't market yourself effectively because your life goals are unclear?

The Terrible Ten Mistakes

HEART & SOUL TIP

Understand the Terrible Ten and then compare how you would conduct a job search and career tune-up with how you should conduct your job search and career tune-up.

Too often career development is broken down into little bite-sized pieces, making it difficult to see the big picture. By learning the 10 biggest career mistakes, you will not only ascertain the latest trends in job searching, but you will also be able to critically compare how you *have* maintained your career with how you *need to* maintain your career. Let's explore each of the Terrible Ten mistakes in depth:

1. Lack of focus or clear sense of purpose
2. Poor resume and cover letter
3. Failure to pursue more than one lead at a time
4. Incorrect positioning in the market
5. Too broad or narrow a scope for your target job
6. Limited research of potential employers
7. Bad attitude: Feeling entitled to a good job
8. Little or no follow-up
9. Poor interviewing and networking skills
10. Overstating your qualifications

1. Lack of Focus or Clear Sense of Purpose

Living with a mission, or a clear sense of purpose, serves so many valuable functions in life. First, you wake up every morning excited about getting on with your day. You sleep better at night because you're confident that there is no other place you would rather be. You're excited about building and improving your relationships with your loved ones, clients, and co-workers. In

HEART & SOUL TIP

Living with a mission, or a clear sense of purpose, serves many valuable functions in life.

your job or job search, you are committed and passionately driven to make your job a special one. Instead of feeling drained and tired all the time, you feel invigorated and passionate! This is the true Heart & Soul way to approach your career.

Beth Johnson

Beth was a bright, hardworking woman with no particular mission or clear sense of purpose. On the surface, she seemed like a lost soul with regard to her career, but we knew that we just had to help her find the right path. During our initial interview, Beth indicated that although she'd been working in retail for a number of years, she was interested in getting a job in pharmaceutical sales. After more questioning, we determined that the only reason she wanted to get the pharmaceutical sales job was that she'd heard it paid well. She admitted she had no passion for or interest in the industry as a whole. She said she was just tired of the low pay in retail and wanted to make some money.

Beth's desire to earn a better income had stifled her true self. She had lost her passion for life and a career because she had chosen to chase this high-paying job for no particular reason besides money. The apathy was written all over her face. She didn't want to think about her future, and she didn't want to go beat the streets looking for a new career. Beth had no real motivation to succeed in her job search beyond the fact that she needed more cash!

Your mission is not an outline of every job you will have for the next 15 years. It's a set of meaningful concepts and/or ideas about who you are and what you want to accomplish at the most fundamental level. Your mission might be one sentence long, or it might be a page long. Your mission is your higher purpose, the reason you're here on Earth. It's what you were born to do in this life. It's the Heart & Soul reason for your existence.

Your mission is something you will probably never fully accomplish or achieve, but it's something you should always work toward. It is your life's highest purpose. Don't worry if you have never prepared any sort of mission.

HEART & SOUL TIP

Although you may never fully achieve your life's mission, you should continually work toward it, setting new goals all along the way.

We'll show you what a few of our clients have prepared and the exciting jobs they found during their most recent job searches. The following table lists a few of our clients, their missions, and the type of work they love.

When you define your purpose, your life takes on new meaning. Your life and career path become clearer, and your search for the perfect job and career becomes much more defined. You're looking for a job that will mean something to you, and if you get paid for doing what you love, all the better!

When you define your purpose, your life takes on new meaning. Your life and career path become clearer, and your job search becomes much more

Client	Mission	Work They Love
Luke	"To educate and entertain."	Computer training
Coren	"To change or increase the world's perceived value of the Earth, its resources, and its climate."	Greenpeace
Thomas	"To lead and nurture my family in both a practical and a spiritual sense."	Life insurance sales (flexible work schedule for family)
Mary	"To promote universal love, self-respect, and mutual respect."	Counselor and therapist

■ **TABLE 3.1**
Matching Mission and Work

defined. Now, instead of being a broad-based, nebulous sort of job search, your quest for that perfect job becomes more purposeful—with real substance and meaning. You're not just out there looking for someone to pay you some money. You're looking for a job that will mean something of value to you, and if you get paid for doing what you love, all the better!

We know how easy it is to start a job search before really thinking about what you want out of life. Sunday morning, you know you're ready for a change; flipping through the want ads, and you see a job that sounds really cool. Then you see another job that also sounds cool. But wait, there's another. If each is a different kind of job, you'll need a totally different resume for each one!

At one time or another, we have probably all dropped a few resumes in the mail without any forethought, but we want to remind you to use caution with any spontaneous job searches—especially those that take you out of your existing profession. Early rejection can be very demoralizing and may provoke you to discount a viable career path too soon. Although there may be a big discrepancy between what you want to do and what you are skilled or trained to do, you need to start bridging that gap. You need to prepare yourself for a time when you will be in a better position to get what you want.

Don't live your life by the motto "If you don't know where you're going, then you're already there." Making any change in your life is going to take focus and commitment, and this is especially true in a career tune-up or job search. Lack of focus or clear sense of purpose is, by far, the greatest job-searching mistake on our Terrible Ten list. Don't let it happen to you!

Now complete Worksheet 3.1 to create a mission and a list of jobs that fit in with your mission.

HEART & SOUL TIP

Never respond to a posted job unless you are sure it represents a career path that aligns with your mission.

HEART & SOUL TIP

Although there may be a big discrepancy between what you want to do and what you are skilled or trained to do, you need to start bridging that gap. You need to prepare yourself for a time when you will be in a better position to get what you want.

Write out your mission here.

List a few favorite career/job paths that fit your mission.

■ **WORKSHEET 3.1**
Align Your Career Path with Your Mission

2. Poor Resume and Cover Letter

Have you ever asked a company to "send you some more information" about its product or services? What was your impression of the company after you received the materials? Were you impressed? Did the company send you the information you requested?

During any customer service process there are key times that we call "moment of truth" indicators, when the customer's loyalty is gained or lost. For example, if a customer identifies a problem, he or she will communicate the problem to a company and then judge the service representative's actions as helpful and appropriate or not. At this "moment of truth," the service rep will earn the customer's loyalty for a long time or lose it forever.

HEART & SOUL TIP

Writing a resume is an art. Your resume must reflect your heart and soul.

When your resume and cover letter are received by an employer, the brief time after the envelope is opened and your materials are scanned is your "moment of truth." That resume is either going into the trash, into the bottomless file cabinet, or on the list of prospects to call to set up an interview.

It's important that you respect this moment of truth and invest heavily in your written presentations. Even if the person to whom you are addressing the resume and letter knows you, your information will surely be passed around to other decision makers who don't know you.

Most people are pretty good about realizing the need for a good resume. A common problem, however, is that many people don't know what makes the best resume for their particular situation. Writing a resume is as much an art as a science. Your resume should follow some basic guidelines and parameters, but beyond that you want your resume to stand out from the competition.

Our intention is not to teach you how to write a high-impact resume and letter, but to make you aware of the importance of doing so. If your resume and cover letter need work, may we recommend our first book in the *Heart & Soul* series, *Heart & Soul Resumes* (Davies-Black Publishing, 1998). This book is available at many retail and online bookstores.

3. Failure to Pursue More than One Lead at a Time

Have you ever been so close to landing a good job that you didn't feel like prospecting for more opportunities? It took so long to get to the job offer stage that you couldn't bear the thought of going through the whole "dog and pony show" again, of finding more potential employers, sending out more resumes, making more follow-up calls, and all the rest of it. You just knew you were going to get the offer soon. You could imagine yourself in the job, and you loved it! Your enthusiasm for the new job was high and you decided to wait for the offer before you did any more job searching. Days went by, weeks went by—you waited and waited and waited. Finally, two months after the interview, you got the call you'd been waiting for, but to your dismay, you heard that although they loved you and still wanted you, due to budget cuts they had a hiring freeze and they would call you at the beginning of the year.

What a blow! You were so ready for that job! You were glad to know that they still wanted you but destroyed by the fact that they were putting the position on hold for a year. You couldn't wait a year, though; you needed a good job now! At that point, you realized that you had no other job opportunities on the table . . . nothing. You hadn't even talked to another company in two months. What were you going to do?

Well, here's what many people would do. First they'd be angry for not getting the offer, and then they'd feel despondent and self-pitying because things just "never go their way." Then they'd feel apathetic because they couldn't control anything in their life, so they might as well just let stuff happen to them. Then they'd muster up some courage and send out some more resumes, do some more follow-up, and eventually get a decent job offer, months later than when they hoped they'd get it!

To avoid the usual heartache, keep in mind these three rules about receiving a job offer: Until you (1) have worked for a company for at least two weeks, (2) received your first paycheck, and (3) received an initial positive response to your work, you don't really have a new job! Unless these three criteria are met, you are officially still in the job market. We hear too many horror stories of promises never filled or commitments never made. So until you are absolutely sure about a new job, you should put 100 percent of your efforts into your continued job-seeking efforts.

> **HEART & SOUL TIP**
>
> *Once you know what you want to do, flood the market with resumes and networking calls. Never, never, never wait for one job lead at a time!*

CAREER SUCCESS STORY

Craig Coruthers

Craig Coruthers burst into our office to tell us that he had an "awesome job offer." Excited for him, we asked him to tell us about it. He talked about the great pay and benefits and all the exciting work he'd be doing. He said he had to move to Atlanta, but he was excited about living in a new city.

After the celebration subsided, he quickly mentioned that they couldn't give him an offer in writing, but they would be glad to e-mail a brief summary of the offer to him. We asked him if he would have to carry the cost of moving himself and his family to Atlanta. He said yes he would, but the company would reimburse him. The more Craig talked about the company and the offer, the more he realized that there was something odd going on. "Why wouldn't they give me a written offer?" he asked. "Is that a big deal?"

What started as a fun celebration turned into a deep conversation about what Craig should do. He was in a quandary, and rightly so. The offer was great—it was just what he was looking for, but he had been burned before by another employer and was concerned about the true intentions of this company. We talked for a long time and Craig decided that unless they could provide a written and enforceable offer, he would have to say no to the deal.

We saw Craig a few months later, and he said he hadn't taken the job because the company would never commit to a written offer. In the next sentence, he laughed as he told us how the company had filed for bankruptcy just last week, and how glad he was that he hadn't taken the job.

Waiting around for one or two job leads to come through for you is a big mistake. If you want your job search to go as quickly as possible, you need to be relentless in your pursuit of a new job. You should never make assumptions about what an employer will offer you or when the offer will be made. You should be networking and sending out resumes the same day that you get an offer—even one from your favorite company.

Intuitively, we know this sounds nuts, but believe us because we know what works—and what doesn't. Even if an offer that's on the table comes through and you accept the job, you still may want to squeeze out a few more interviews with other companies during your first few weeks of employment. It's interesting to notice the response you get from potential employers when you tell them you are thinking about accepting an offer from a competing company. It seems to make them want you that much more. If you play it right, you can parlay your one success into many. So long as you treat everyone professionally, it is perfectly ethical to "play" the companies off one another to try to get the best offer you can.

4. Incorrect Positioning in the Marketplace

We've noticed that, for the most part, recent graduates and "downsized professionals" tend to overestimate their value, or position, in the marketplace, and those reentering the workforce after an extended absence tend to underestimate their value. We know that these generalizations, of course, are not true for everyone, and we know that each person's situation is unique. But you should keep these tips in mind as you consider your worth and position in the job market.

You must have a clear idea of what you are worth in the marketplace. If you don't know your worth, your job search will be unclear and unfocused. For example, if you believe you're worth a guaranteed salary of $100,000 a year, ask yourself why. Who else do you know with similar skills and experience who makes that kind of money? On the other hand, if you think you are worth only $15,000 a year, you'd better be sure that you are not estimating too low. If you overestimate your value, you're going to have a hard time finding the work you love; if you underestimate your value, you may get a job quickly, but you'll likely be working far below your skill and competence level.

HEART & SOUL TIP

Overvaluing yourself in the workplace could price you out of jobs and leave you with no job offers. Undervaluing yourself in the workplace could result in a less than average job and money still left on the table.

"Doogie" James

A sharply dressed, confident young man, 20 years old, strutted into our office and demanded that we provide a list of target employers for him. Although Doogie isn't his real name, we assigned him the nickname because of his precocious manner (after the television character), after he arrogantly barked out his credentials and told us that he didn't need any career or job search help because he could get a job anywhere he wanted. He told us he expected to be offered $80,000 a year.

He illustrated his point by explaining that he had competed against many of his college peers to win a highly coveted life insurance sales job. He said he won the job over thousands of others and he could do it again with any company he chose.

Our first thought was to congratulate this insurance company for enticing so many college graduates to want to compete for such a position. Traditionally, recruiting for that kind of position is difficult. For that matter, we felt that any company that could create such a buzz about its service or product was doing a great job!

We offered Doogie our assistance, but he declined, and we wondered why he had sought us out in the first place. We knew his confidence would serve him well in a challenging sales job. Because rejection is commonplace in sales, Doogie would need to confront it head-on day after day. However, we worried for him because if his confidence was just a mask to cover some insecurity, we knew he was in for a long, hard haul in his job search and career. And with his expectations so high, we were concerned that he might have priced himself out of a job—especially a job suitable for a new graduate.

On the other side of the coin, we have worked with many mothers, for example, who have left good jobs to take care of their children. After a 5-to-10-year absence from the workforce, many moms are excited to get back to work again and are not too ambitious in their salary expectations. An employer is quick to recognize a good deal and will snatch up a sharp candidate in a heartbeat if the person has below-market income expectations. Often, the resulting employment turns out to be unfulfilling and not rewarding for the employee.

The resolution to this Terrible Ten mistake is relatively easy and painless: Educate yourself! Too often people with inappropriate salary expectations learn of their mistake too late—after they have already interviewed with a good potential employer and made an impression. Don't let this happen to you! Before you send out one resume or start your career tune-up in any way, determine what you want to do and how much (in a range) you need and expect to be paid.

So how do you find this information? Try the Internet. The federal government compiles vast amounts of data on wages in industries and states, and this information may be of great assistance to you, especially in your preliminary stages of research. Visit the United States Department of Labor's Web site at http://www.dol.gov to orient yourself to basic wage levels in your area and chosen industry. You might also search the Internet for local and state Web sites that compile similar information. This form of research is great, but you can go further: The best way to get the information you want is to talk to the right people.

Make a list of friends and colleagues who will have no influence in hiring you for your next job. These people can talk openly with you, without your worrying about saying anything "right" or "wrong." Try to get an idea of what people in a similar situation and experience level are getting paid. Then do some networking and visit with people in more influential positions—on a casual, informational level. Ask pertinent questions that can help you determine what you're worth. You'll probably have to be very tactful while doing this research to avoid asking questions about privileged information, but this is important information you must have in your job search.

If you find that a particular career path pays a wage that's too low for you, you can cancel that search before wasting a single stamp mailing out a resume. If you hear that another choice career pays more than you expected, your worth expectations can go up for that career path!

Use Worksheet 3.2 to categorize your various career options and compare your income expectations with what you researched to be true and accurate. Remember to research salaries for people in employment situations that are similar to your own.

Possible Career Path	Salary Expectations	Actual Market Salary

■ **WORKSHEET 3.2**
Compare Your Salary Expectations with Actual Data

5. Too Broad or Narrow a Scope for Your Target Job

This mistake is a classic blunder in the job-seeking game. If you're considering too many different jobs, you won't be focused enough to be successful. If you are focused on only one specific kind of job, you're limiting yourself and may miss other potential opportunities.

Betsy Long

CAREER SUCCESS STORY

Betsy, a lab technician at a clinical trial lab, wanted a new career. She came to us for advice about what sort of job(s) she should target. After months of unsuccessful job-seeking attempts, she just couldn't find anything she wanted. We asked what kinds of opportunities she had been targeting, and she listed five jobs in the medical profession, three jobs not in the medical profession, and seven companies that she admired and would like to work for.

After further discussion, we determined that Betsy had a clear sense of purpose in her life and her career focus was shaping up well. But she had too many different career and job paths to consider. Every time she added another career path, she added an hour of job search work to her day! She was overwhelmed with searching for a job and she had spread herself too thin. Each career or profession has its own contacts and decision makers, and to network and build relationships with too many different people in different occupations is too large a task to accomplish with any sort of depth.

By targeting similar career paths and job options, you create a synergy in your job search. For example, we suggested to Betsy that she prioritize her career options and target only the top few positions in closely related fields. By doing this, she would narrow the scope of her job search, and her base of contacts to network with would shrink to a much more manageable size. As a result, she would feel much less overwhelmed and confused about the search process.

HEART & SOUL TIP

By targeting similar career paths and job options, you create a synergy in your job search.

Judy Banks

CAREER SUCCESS STORY

Judy Banks had a much simpler goal. She wanted to be an animal trainer in a major zoo somewhere in South Carolina, Georgia, or Florida. She was very credible, too. Her experience was impeccable and her salary expectations were right on the mark. She told us that she had already talked to people at the zoos she knew about, but none of them had any current openings.

With so few potential employers, she had already done everything she could do. So we encouraged her to broaden the scope of her target job. Could she consider zoos in other states? Could she consider other jobs that would appre-

HEART & SOUL TIP

If your job search is too narrowly focused, you may want to consider opening your options and thereby increase your opportunities and chances of success!

ciate her experience as an animal trainer? We wanted to open her mind to other options because if she wanted a job quickly, she was going to have to consider alternative job paths. We reminded her that taking another related job would not negate future animal-training opportunities. In fact, she could still continue to network with her favorite zoos, so when a position did come open, she would be first in line to apply!

6. Limited Research of Potential Employers

Nine times out of ten, job seekers don't know specifically what companies to target. But how can you embark on a successful job search if you don't have all the pertinent companies in your database? Often, job seekers will target a few widely known companies, but no more. What a waste! Small and medium-sized businesses are by far the highest-growth employers in the country. To avoid this mistake, you need a good database of all the employers in your target area.

At the Heart & Soul Career Center, we maintain a database of more than 10 million employers in the United States. Your local or online bookstore also has many books that list employers by various categories. You can find companies

by location, industry, size, years in business, and type of ownership. Through the Web and other resources, you have access to all the information you need to find the employers you want!

Our clients define their target employer in general terms— usually by industry, size, and location. If we know this information, we can come up with an amazingly accurate and well-defined target list of employers. Size and location are not that difficult to determine, and this information can really help you hone in on a manageable list of companies.

The more difficult part in researching employers is defining the appropriate industries to target. On the following page is the SIC (Standard Industry Code) list. This is how the government and most databases categorize types of businesses. Try to find your target industry classifications in the list. Visit your library or local career center for a more in-depth list of industry codes.

Although the SIC can be helpful, it does have an inherent problem for you as you research industry careers. For example, if you wanted to be a plant manager for a wood processing plant, what industry would you choose? Probably #24 Manufacturing: Lumber and Wood Products, right? That is pretty easy to get to. But what if you were in sales? How would you define your industry? Using the SIC, you can't. Sales is a profession that is transferable across many industry lines. First, you must define what kind of sales you want to target— Tangible Goods, or Not Tangible Goods? Retail or Wholesale?

Agriculture, Forestry, Fishing (01–09)
Agricultural Production Crops (01)
Agricultural Production Livestock (02)
Agricultural Services (07)
Forestry (08)
Fishing, Hunting, Trapping (09)

Mining (10–14)
Metal Mining (10)

Construction (15–17)
General Building Contractors (15)
Heavy Construction, except Building (16)
Special Trade Construction (17)

Manufacturing (20–39)
Food and Drink Products (20)
Textile Mill Products (22)
Apparel and Other Textile Products (23)
Lumber and Wood Products (24)
Furniture and Fixtures (25)
Paper and Allied Products (26)
Printing and Publishing (27)
Chemicals and Allied Products (28)
Petroleum and Coal Products (29)
Rubber and Misc. Plastic Products (30)
Leather and Leather Products (31)
Stone, Clay, and Glass Products (32)
Primary Metal Industries (33)
Fabricated Metals Products (34)
Industrial Machinery and Equipment (35)
Electronic and Other Equipment (36)
Transportation Equipment (37)
Instruments and Related Products (38)
Misc. Manufacturing (39)

Transportation, Communication, Utilities (40–49)
Railroad Transportation (40)
Local Passenger Transit (41)
Trucking and Warehousing (42)
United States Postal Service (43)
Water Transportation (44)
Transportation by Air (45)
Pipelines, except Natural Gas (46)
Transportation Services (47)
Communication (48)
Electric, Gas, and Sanitary Services (49)

Wholesale Trade (50–51)
Wholesale Trade Durable Goods (50)
Wholesale Trade Nondurable Goods (51)

Retail Trade (52–59)
Building Materials/Garden Supplies (52)
General Merchandise Stores (53)
Food Stores (54)
Automotive Dealers and Service Stations (55)
Apparel and Accessory Stores (56)
Furniture and Home Furnishing (57)
Eating and Drinking Places (58)
Misc. Retail (59)

Finance, Insurance, and Real Estate (60–67)
Depository Institutions (60)
Nondepository Institutions (61)
Security and Commodity Brokers (62)
Insurance Carriers (63)
Insurance Agents, Brokers, and Services (64)
Real Estate (65)
Holding and Other Investment Offices (67)

Services (70–89)
Hotels and Other Lodging Places (70)
Personal Services (72)
Business Services (73)
Auto Repair, Services, and Parking (75)
Misc. Repair Services (76)
Motion Pictures (78)
Amusement and Recreation Services (79)
Health Services (80)
Legal Services (81)
Educational Services (82)
Social Services (83)
Museums, Botanicals, Zoological Gardens (84)
Membership Organizations (86)
Engineering and Management Services (87)
Private Households (88)
Misc. Services (89)

Public Administration (91–99)
Executive, Legislative, and General (91)
Justice, Public Order, and Safety (92)
Finance Taxation and Monetary Policy (93)
Administration of Human Resources (94)
Environmental, Quality, and Housing (95)
Administration of General Economic Programs (96)
National Security and International Affairs (97)
Nonclassifiable Establishments (99)

■ **TABLE 3.1**
Standard Industry Codes

Jimmy Jennings

Jimmy was a sales manager with a large national appliance consumer service chain. He assured us that he liked his profession, but he had been let go amid a recent company buyout. He said he would be willing to consider any kind of sales; it didn't matter what kind of sales position he got, so long as it paid well. Jimmy was a powerful salesperson and he could probably get a job with almost any company he wanted. However, from a marketability standpoint, his job search would be much quicker if he targeted a type of business that was similar to what he had been doing before.

So we narrowed his industry criteria down to #72 Personal Services and #73 Business Services. The companies we found were perfect for Jimmy's experience selling retail services. Whether he would be selling to businesses or consumers was not relevant, and he should consider both categories.

Sometimes researching employers by industry is easy, and sometimes it's not quite so obvious. Many occupations, like sales, exist in many types of industries. Assuming that all the potential industries fall in line with your personal mission, you should consider only those that enhance your marketability and speed your success.

HEART & SOUL TIP

You will more than likely be most successful finding a career in an industry in which you have some experience or exposure.

7. Bad Attitude: Feeling Entitled to a Good Job

Have you ever felt like this?

"They owe me."

"If I don't land this job, they must be idiots."

"How dare they not offer me the job."

"I can get any job I want."

This job-seeking blunder is simply about maintaining a proper attitude. If you are overly confident, you may come across as though you think you are entitled to the job. We've seen this in people after a few too many job rejections or just as they try to change career paths. They tend to "pump" themselves up to help build a false sense of self-confidence; the result is that they make themselves believe they are better than what the job market is telling them. It's like an internal motivational pep talk has boosted their egos but done nothing to improve their marketability.

Sometimes personnel from large bureaucratic organizations fall into this trap as well. They are accustomed to working within the tight constraints of a big institution, but they can be thrown off guard by the fiercely competitive nature of the job search in the private sector. Their reaction seems to be one of entitlement, and their actions are sometimes interpreted as brash arrogance.

There is no place for a bad attitude in a job search, no matter what your situation or history is. Sometimes people project arrogance to cover up some insecurity; others simply may not know any better. We occasionally interview people who appear at first to be arrogant, but upon further investigation, we usually learn that they are putting up a front because they believe "that is how all businesspeople act"! (We tell them they've been watching too much TV!) Good business is not about being arrogant. It's about building relationships and maintaining boundaries. We urge you to be poised, competitive, and confident in your job search, but be very aware of the tone and attitude you present in an interview or a networking situation as well as on a day-to-day basis. Remember to utilize Heart & Soul techniques throughout your day to help you—including meditation.

HEART & SOUL TIP

Be careful of feeling that you are entitled to the best job. This will almost ensure failure. Be poised, competitive, and confident in your job search, but be aware of the tone and attitude you present.

Too often, we focus our lives on ways to be more productive and make more money. In our ambitious quest, we tend to forget the important things in our lives—family, friendship, health, and other things. Just as important as living with your mission and goals is enjoying your life in the moment and being humbly grateful for your loved ones and the things that you value most! This is the way you live a true Heart & Soul life.

Think about driving to your favorite distant destination. You plot your course on a map, plan your trip, and then go. What do you do in the car to make your trip enjoyable? You stop and sightsee or visit places that are interesting to you. You may play games with your kids, or you may enjoy a deep conversation with a friend. The last thing you want to do is monitor the clock on a long trip to see how far you've gone. That makes the trip last forever!

HEART & SOUL TIP

Think of your career as a long journey. You can enjoy the ride, or you can watch the clock to see when you will arrive.

You've set your career on course and are currently seeking work that will launch your career in the right direction. If you focus only on getting the next great job, your attitude will be awful. Be confident that your job search will eventually be a success and take care of your emotional well-being on an ongoing basis. When your attitude is right and you feel good about yourself, then success will find you!

In our book *Heart & Soul Resumes*, we talk about maintaining an "attitude of gratitude." If you are the kind of person who tends to err on the side of overconfidence, we recommend making a list of everything you are grateful for. This simple little exercise makes you look at your life from a new perspective. At the other extreme, if you tend to err on the side of low self-esteem, this exercise can help boost your morale and crystallize your vision of the great person you really are!

Use Worksheet 3.3 on the next page to write down all the people and things you're grateful for. As you do this, feel the stress melt away. Feel how your feelings of arrogance and entitlement get replaced with a strong, yet humbling, sense of yourself and a new determination to make your career goals work.

WHAT ARE YOU GRATEFUL FOR?

1.

2.

3.

4.

5.

6.

7.

8.

9.

10.

11.

12.

13.

14.

15.

■ **WORKSHEET 3.3**
What Are You Grateful For?

8. Little or No Follow-Up

Everyone hates to follow up with phone calls after sending resumes. But you should know that follow-up is one of the most fundamental pieces of a successful job search.

CAREER
ROAD
BLOCK
STORY

Fred Henries

Fred called us to help him in his job search. He said he was focused and driven and wanted to pursue a career in industrial chemical sales. After sending out 500 resumes to all the right people in all the right companies, he said he was thoroughly disappointed with the abysmal results. "Not a single positive call," he complained. "I received 25 rejection letters and not a single positive call, even six months after I sent out my resumes."

Fred's work experience was strong but not exactly related to industrial chemical sales. We could see how chemical companies might not understand why Fred wanted to change careers. All the "players" in the industry seemed to know each other, and Fred might be seen as an outsider. We were surprised that Fred did not get a good response from his campaign because his resume and letter looked great. So we asked, "Fred, what was the general response you got when you followed up with all those companies you targeted on the phone?"

Sheepishly, Fred admitted that he hadn't made any follow-up calls. "Is it too late to call them now?" he asked.

Fred put together a great job search campaign but never finished it. He told us that he hated cold calls and just never got around to calling those companies back.

Employers can get hundreds of resumes (or more) in any given month. Imagine how difficult it is for your resume to get noticed when it's buried in a huge stack of resumes. If you make a follow-up call, however, at least an employer might pull your resume out of the stack and take a look. After you send that resume, make sure you make a follow-up phone call!

You've got to aggressively and consistently follow up in your job searching efforts. Follow up after informal networking meetings, formal interviews, and after you send a resume. Follow up after any important contact you make with an influential person or decision maker. Make yourself stand out above the rest. Your skills and credentials will get you so far, but at some point you need to initiate some meaningful conversation, be it in the form of follow-up calls or face-to-face meetings.

HEART & SOUL TIP

You should be fully prepared and expect to make a follow-up call to each company that received your resume.

9. Poor Interviewing and Networking Skills

If you had to choose only one job search skill that you could excel at, interviewing and networking skills would be it! It's a huge mistake to be ill prepared for an interview or an important networking meeting. Be prepared to know what to say when you're finally in front of the right decision maker.

CAREER
SUCCESS
STORY

Amy Preit

Amy, a second-year MBA student, was looking for a career position for after she graduated in the coming spring. She desperately wanted to be a consultant. Before we met her, she had already had dealings with a major consulting firm. She had had an initial telephone-screening interview that had gone horribly, and she knew she needed help so she would do better with other interviews for consulting positions.

Amy said her problem was that she felt unprepared for the interview and was immediately caught off-guard when the interviewer asked the first question: "What do you want to do with our firm?"

Amy told us she had wanted to say, "Whatever you've got." Amy's intentions were to get in the door to do any sort of consulting work. She couldn't really say what kind of consulting work she wanted because she wasn't sure what the firm did. Later in the interview, Amy was asked to describe her work experience and career goals. Amy said she had just rambled through what she thought were good answers.

With Amy's help, we focused our efforts on two areas for improvement. The first was geared toward improving her ability to answer generic interview questions primarily related to herself and her goals. The second area was geared toward understanding the company and learning how to research an employer before the initial interview ever begins.

Worksheet 3.4 presents a list of common interview and networking questions. While the exact phrasing of the questions will be different in your interviews, their content and message will be similar. As we recommended to Amy, write out your answer to each one and commit it to memory. Our intent is not to have you regurgitate the same answer verbatim but for you to be able to clearly articulate who you are and what you want to accomplish.

On the other hand, networking skills require that you proactively seek out influential people, hiring authorities, business owners, and people who know these people. Once you locate a key person, you can call him or her and request an informal meeting on the phone, via e-mail, over lunch, or wherever you feel most comfortable. The most difficult part of networking is not only answering questions well (as you do in an interview) but also asking the right questions.

COMMON INTERVIEW QUESTIONS

Here are some general guidelines to help you in answering interview and networking questions. Always accentuate the positive. If you are asked a negative question, answer it directly, but follow up with comments toward the positive. For example, you might be asked, "What is your worst trait?" Your answer could be, "My worst trait was 'such and such,' but during the past year I have received training and experience that have helped me improve my skills dramatically." You could also answer with a "negative" trait that would be appealing to the employer: "I work too hard."

Illustrate your answers with real-life stories. Nothing communicates your message better than a good story. Which do you think is more powerful? "I am an excellent salesperson. I always make my goals." Or, "Sales is my strong suit. Last year, for example, my boss put me in a territory with no existing accounts. During the year I built my new territory into the highest-producing territory in the company, achieving more than $25 million." An illustration of your accomplishments tells so much more than just a list of your skills.

Prepare well for the open-ended question. Many conversations and interviews begin with a broad, open-ended request, such as, "Tell me about yourself." This is your time to shine. You get to show how well you control a conversation in addition to giving appropriate information about yourself. Your listener will measure you on how quickly you answer the question and how well you impart relevant information.

Write out a script for yourself using the questions below. Keep it short. Start with the basics like education and work history. Tell several stories of your greatest accomplishments. Give your listener a sense of your career direction, and if you choose, close with something personal—like your interests or hobbies. Practice this out loud until you have it down. You will use this same "script" time and time again.

Tell me about yourself.

What are your long-term goals?

What are your short-term goals?

How do you plan to achieve both your short-term and long-term goals?

Tell me about your hobbies.

What are your greatest strengths?

What are your greatest weaknesses?

What was your favorite job and why?

Describe a situation where you had a conflict with a co-worker and how you handled it.

What do you think people like most about you?

What do you think people like least about you?

How well do you work under pressure?

How do you motivate people?

Describe your leadership style.

What is the most important lesson you have learned in or out of school?

Who do you admire most in your life and why?

What accomplishments are you most proud of?

What characteristics do you think are most important in this position?

Why do you think you're the best person for this job?

■ **WORKSHEET 3.4 CONTINUED**
Preparing for Interviewing and Networking Conversations

Following is a list of questions that you may want to ask in a networking situation. Don't limit yourself to this list. Think up several questions that are appropriate to the person you're meeting with. If you need more help with your interviewing and networking skills, check out our last book, *Heart & Soul Internet Job Search* (Davies-Black Publishing, 1999).

- What political or economic changes will affect your industry in the coming years?
- What are the best companies to watch for in this industry?
- Do you know of any employer that is hiring or planning to hire soon?
- Do you know any hiring decision makers with these employers?
- May I use your name when I call these decision makers?
- What is the greatest threat to your industry right now?
- Do you know a few other people who might help me gather information for my job search?

Think of your own networking questions as well!

10. Overstating Your Qualifications

We'll start by asking a few questions. Let's see how you do on our Heart & Soul career tune-up quiz.

- What is your most "lied about" qualification on a resume?
- Is it OK to lie to get a job as long you don't think it will hurt anyone or you won't get caught?
- Is it OK to exaggerate your skills and qualifications on a resume with the intention of telling the truth only if someone asks a direct or pointed question?
- Is it OK to downplay potentially negative issues until you get in the door, and then reveal your weaknesses gradually and tactfully so you don't lose the job offer?

In our own subtle and calm way, let us tell you how we feel: NEVER LIE ABOUT YOUR QUALIFICATIONS! You will only get yourself into trouble. Whether the employer is checking references before you get a formal offer or your lies are discovered a year after you begin working, lies will severely damage your reputation, credibility, and marketability.

We're not suggesting that you would actually lie. Anyone who would buy a Heart & Soul book is probably not the type to lie. But the fact remains that many people do, and it's a temptation you should resist! What's more, it's not necessary. Here's how we suggest you answer the questions above:

- Never lie. It's wrong, unethical, and potentially very damaging to you and your potential employer.
- Don't exaggerate with the intention of telling the truth only if you're "caught." You're still lying.
- Do downplay negative issues. Always put your best foot forward. You can be more open about your weaknesses once you are "in the door." If you have some bad points (or skeletons in the closet), it's best to downplay them until you can establish a good working relationship. You can be more free with your information as the interview process goes on. Up front, though, you can't afford to emphasize anything negative.

The Terrible Ten job-seeking mistakes illustrated in this chapter represent 99 percent of the job-losing blunders that take place in the market today. Take time to analyze your job search plan, and make sure your skills are up to par.

Stressing for Success

Life is a grindstone, and whether it grinds you down
or polishes you up is for you and you alone to decide.

CAVETT ROBERT

*T*HERE'S PROBABLY NOT A person alive who hasn't been "stressed out" at some point. That's just the way life is. But what you do with that stress makes all the difference in the world. You can wallow around in it, get sucked into it so deeply that it suffocates you, and drown in it. Or you can use this stressful energy in a positive way and turn it into an opportunity.

You'll encounter many "problems" in today's career world. But turn the problems around and you've got opportunities. Our fourth never-before-published secret to capturing Heart & Soul in your work life, "Understand the common career stress trigger points for success," is one of our most vital strategies for a true synergistic Heart & Soul career tune-up.

There are many reasons we stress out. Demanding jobs and work environments, personal relationships, money problems, health problems, too many responsibilities—all of these are contributing factors to stress. However, the primary and most consistent stress factors of all time are career related, which include changing or losing a job. Perhaps you have a good job but it isn't making you happy.

Perhaps your work environment doesn't suit your personality. Perhaps you're not making as much money as you'd like. Career problems are a part of our everyday lives, and whether large or small, they can cause stress. And stress, if not used in a positive way, can take a toll on your health and your life. As you already know, stress is the culprit that causes many heart attacks and sleepless nights, and as a general rule, it simply wreaks havoc in your life. But it doesn't have to.

We exist day-to-day in our world of stress without realizing what that stress is all about. We accept it as a part of life and seldom try to do anything constructive with it. That's where the Heart & Soul approach comes into play. By using a Heart & Soul approach to stress, you can change each moment. You can change each day, and you can change your career. In fact, you can change your life.

HEART & SOUL TIP

Stress is a form of energy and can be used in a positive way.

If stress is running rampant and out of control in your life, then how can you succeed? To successfully "tune up" your career, you must know what to do with your stress.

Most people don't realize that stress is a form of energy. Think about it. When you're stressed out, it's hard to sit still and relax. It's hard to get to the inner you where all your wonderful, creative thought processes and dreams are germinating. Your mind is zooming at a thousand miles per second as you worry, chew your fingernails, clutch your stomach, eat incessantly to calm your nerves, or just pace the floor. Or, perhaps you just become immobile. Too much powerful stress can overwhelm you to the point where you just freeze. You're so stressed out that you simply can't move. We all have felt this way at one time or another.

Think Positive Thoughts

HEART & SOUL TIP

You can stress for success!

If you let stress get the upper hand, you're using your stress energy in a negative way. But you don't have to. You can take this energy and use it in a positive way. You can actually "stress for success," which we'll explore in depth in this chapter.

CAREER
SUCCESS
STORY

Mark Weafer

Our client Mark Weafer's experience is a clear example of how stress can be used to achieve success. Mark turned his problems into opportunities.

In the early 1970s, when Mark was just 26 years old, he was selling large geodesic domes in New York and making $2 million a year. At the time, Mark was selling these domes as quickly as they could be built! He was an executive salesman—he wore the finest clothes, ate at the fanciest restaurants, and drove the most luxurious cars. He was at the top of the world.

However, Mark's life was about to be turned upside down. The domes were made out of polyvinylchloride (PVC), a petrochemical (plastic) product. In 1974, the first Arab oil embargo would change his life forever.

When OPEC was formed, the price of petroleum products skyrocketed. As oil prices soared and affected both the production and cost of the PVC domes, Mark's sales plummeted and he eventually found himself declaring bankruptcy. The stress of losing his job and filing for bankruptcy took its toll on him initially. He explained that he got physically sick from all the stress. He was letting the stress consume his life. He went to bed at 6:00 P.M. and slept until 6:00 A.M. Fleeing from the world, he used sleep as an escape.

Mark had hit rock bottom. He drove an old car. He worked at odd jobs—unloading products off railroad cars in New York's freezing winter weather wearing a London Fog trench coat, a fine suit, and leather shoes (the only clothes the bankruptcy court had left him), and earning little more than a whopping $2 an hour. In the geodesic dome business, Mark had been a super salesman. Now he felt like a total failure.

Mark knew he was at the very bottom. Things couldn't get much worse. It was being at the bottom that made him start over. It made Mark realize that he didn't have to stay at the bottom. He didn't have to dwell on his failures and his poverty. In other words, he decided to use his stress as a way to improve himself and his situation.

HEART & SOUL TIP

There's always a positive way to solve your problems. Use stress in a positive way to achieve success.

Inspired by motivational tapes, Mark realized that he loved to speak in front of people and wanted to encourage others to pursue happiness and success as a way of life. He decided to pursue a career in professional speaking, writing, and entrepreneuring, and built his life to be the successful one it is today. He took his problems and stress and decided to do something about them. Mark saw his problems as opportunities instead of stumbling blocks, and he used his stress in a positive way to achieve success.

Following is another example of someone who used stress to achieve success after looking at her problems objectively and deciding to put her stress energy into action.

Samantha Robinson

Samantha Robinson walked into our office and said, "I was laid off two months ago from my position as a fitness coordinator at Central Hospital. I need a job and I'm not sure what to do."

About 35 years old, Samantha was tall and slim and looked like the type of person who would be in physical fitness because of her superb physique. However, her demeanor and slouch made it apparent that she wasn't feeling very positive or confident that day. "What, exactly, is the problem?" we asked her.

"I've been so stressed out that I can't motivate myself to look for a job," she continued. "I can't sleep at night because I'm worried, and I can't find a job because I don't really know what to do. I have so much to do to prepare my resume, find job contacts, and stuff like that—I just feel numb!"

We reviewed and updated her resume and then counseled her on her job search strategies. We emphasized to Samantha that she could be using this stress energy to help her look for a new job. We outlined a plan for her, detailing her schedule.

HEART & SOUL TIP

Use your stress energy to look for jobs!

Sample Day Schedule

7:30 A.M.	Out of bed and meditate. Get in touch with your inner self, your dreams, and your goals. Have a talk with your spiritual self.
8:00 A.M.	Into the shower.
8:30 A.M.	Get dressed for the day.
9:00 A.M.	Breakfast.
9:30 A.M.	Head out to the library to research companies, or log on to the Internet and search.
12:00 P.M.	Call a friend and have lunch. Enjoy the moment of taking a break from your routine.
1:00 P.M.	Use the afternoon as study and research time. Make a list of contacts and phone calls you need to make. This is a good time to plan your next day's activities.

HEART & SOUL TIP

When looking for a job, it's important to stick to a schedule and to be as productive as possible throughout your day.

This is just a brief example of a schedule that can help you organize your career tune-up. Do you understand how and why we arranged her schedule as we did? Many people get out of their routines when they lose their jobs. As a result, they become unfocused and unmotivated. It's important to stick to a schedule and to be as productive as possible throughout your day.

As Samantha continued with career planning on a daily basis, she focused her stress energy on the job search projects and turned her stress into a positive strategy. She had lots of energy, but without planning and direction, she was

HEART & SOUL TIP

Using stress to achieve success is a positive choice.

immobilized to the point where she couldn't get anything accomplished. When she turned around her attitude and made a positive change, she found the perfect job.

Using your stress to achieve success is a choice—pure and simple. If you're utilizing our Heart & Soul principles in your life, you're choosing to use your stress as a way to succeed, as a way to overcome problems and so-called failures. We emphasize *so-called failures* because we don't believe there are any failures in life, only opportunities. However, if you don't grab that opportunity and focus on turning that stress into positive energy, you won't succeed. You'll stop yourself with your own stressful stumbling blocks, and that can lead to illnesses, unhappiness, and a negative way of living.

You can use stress to achieve success and to overcome life's stumbling blocks in several ways. For example, you can control your moods. Rick Pitino, former head coach for the University of Kentucky basketball program, wrote the book *Success Is a Choice*. In the book, Rick discusses a conversation he had with one of his moodier players. He told the player that his moods could ruin his game and control his life in a negative way. Rick suggested that the player

HEART & SOUL TIP

There are no failures in life—only opportunities.

instead focus his energy on success. Rick used these kinds of tactics to motivate players, which led the team to great success.

Rick believes that being positive in your life on a daily basis is one of the key elements to success—and we agree. Rick has been very successful and continues to be. He has one of the most stressful jobs on the planet, and he uses that stress in a positive way to achieve success for himself and his basketball team.

When we let a bad mood control us, we allow our positive attitude to dwindle downward in a spiral—into an abyss of self-pity. It's easy to do. Sometimes we have to work hard at being positive and controlling our moods. But it's doable. The fact is that our moods greatly enhance or "dehance" our everyday stress.

Athletes talk about the "zone," the state in which they are focused, in the groove, in their comfort zone, with their self-esteem sky high. When an athlete—or anyone in any career field—is in this zone, great things can happen. It's all about being in tune with life—knowing you are exactly where you

HEART & SOUL TIP

Our moods greatly enhance or "dehance" our everyday stress.

should be at exactly the right time. It's being aware of the moment and living that moment to the fullest. This is living in the "zone." And the way to get there is through controlling your moods—staying positive, looking on the bright side. So, when stress spills over into your life, you can take that stress and turn it into positive energy. It's a simple concept but very difficult to maintain every day. With discipline, you can do it. Just pay attention to your moods and your attitudes, and make it a point to change the negative to positive.

Chad Moore

Chad Moore traveled to Chicago to attend an automobile dealership conference. It was early March and sharp winds chilled the night. It reminded him that spring was still a couple of months away.

Scenario One: At the hotel that first night, he called his wife, Maura, and said, "I can't believe how tired I am. What a long day. All those speeches. I thought they would never end. And why are we in Chicago? I hate Chicago. It's too crowded. And all these tall buildings! I heard the other dealership's people are going to the Caribbean. And here we are stuck in cold, windy Chicago. I told you I should have gone to work for them. This is awful."

Scenario Two: Here's Chad in the same situation on the phone with his wife. Notice the difference in his attitude:

"What a great conference. And those speeches. I learned so much, and I know when I get back to work I'm going to be better equipped to do my job. And what a great city—all the music, museums, and culture. I wish I had more time to enjoy them; we'll have to come back here for vacation sometime. Chicago is a great place to have a conference. Those other dealership people have to go all the way to the Caribbean. What a long trip that would be. And you know how I burn in the sun! This is a really great hotel. We have to come back here, Maura!"

These are two different approaches—two different attitudes—to the same situation. The second scenario uses a positive outlook to improve the mood—to take a stressful situation and make it a positive, successful one. Table 4.1 shows how to deal with a stressful situation from two different viewpoints, and the difference a positive attitude makes.

Bad Mood—Negative Attitude Thinking	Good Mood—Positive Attitude Thinking
I have so much work to do. It's just not fair. I'll never get it done.	When I finish all this work, just think of all I will have accomplished. The more work I finish, the more I can get done!
My boss is always giving me extra projects to do. He knows how busy I am!	My boss has a lot of confidence in my ability to complete multiple projects. He has a lot of faith in me. I'm happy that he knows he can depend on me.
Why does everyone want something from me? I'm too busy. Can't they leave me alone?	I'm honored that so many people seek me out for advice. I feel needed.
Oh, no! It's almost 3:00 P.M. and this project is only half done. I still have a ton of work to do.	It's almost 3:00 P.M. and my project is already half done. I think I can finish by 5:00 if I really focus!

■ **TABLE 4.1**
The Difference Attitude Makes

Do you get the idea? You can see the difference in the attitudes and moods of the two different responses. It takes some practice to train yourself to think positively and to keep yourself in a good mood. It takes discipline.

The fact is, we live in a negative world. We are inundated with negative thoughts every day. It takes discipline to control these negative thoughts—to turn a bad mood into a good mood, a frown into a smile. We know you've heard all this before. Numerous motivational speakers talk about this. Yet few people really do anything about it. As a result, too much energy is used up by being negative and wallowing in bad moods. Negativity and bad moods create stressful situations. They create an energy that's powerful and destructive. That's why it's so important to pay attention to your moods and your attitudes, to discipline yourself and think positively. Only then are you on your way to turning that stress into success—into making success a real choice and not just an accident. Actually, there are no accidents, despite what people may think. We are exactly where we're supposed to be, doing exactly what we're supposed to be doing, at all times. Life has been designed this way. We will discuss negativity at length in Chapter 5, "Managing Negativity."

Your attitude controls your life, and it controls your career. It's such a simple part of your everyday existence that you may not pay attention to it. People get grumpy and stay grumpy; they feel bad and allow that feeling to affect everything else in their lives. Many people walk around in a fog—caught up in all that they've been led to believe. Even in their careers, they do what they think they're supposed to. They never realize that they have the power to change everything they think, feel, and do. But the truth is, we all have the power to change our attitude toward life, toward our career, toward everything!

HEART & SOUL TIP

We all have the power to change our attitudes toward life, toward our careers, toward everything!

Think Positively About Others

Another important component of attitude is the way you think and feel about other people. It's not possible to like everyone; we'd be dishonest if we said it was. However, it *is* possible to change the way you view people and to reassess your attitude toward others. It's common to work with people you don't like. Even so, you don't need to let this interfere with your attitude, and you don't need to let it stress you out. Believe it or not, the way you perceive and think about others greatly affects your stress level. Any time you have a negative thought, it enhances stress. Any time you have a positive thought, it "dehances" stress.

On the following four pages are some brief exercises that can help you jump-start your positive thinking. Practice these techniques throughout the day to strengthen your discipline muscles. For these exercises, read the highlighted situations and then write down both positive and negative reactions/thoughts/attitudes. Pay attention to how you feel as you write down each thought. This simple training prepares you to make an adjustment in your thinking, in your own attitude, so you can stress your way to success.

ALTERING YOU ATTITUDE: SCENARIO ONE

You are driving home from work and it's getting late. You didn't want to work this late, but your boss has been hinting that you need to put in extra hours at night and on weekends to succeed in this business. By the time you leave it's very dark. As you're driving down the highway, all of a sudden you hear a "thump, thump, thump" and realize you have a flat tire.

How do you react? Explain the different reactions you COULD have in this situation. Remember, you want to TRAIN yourself to be positive, to be in a good mood, so keep this in mind when writing down your reactions.

Negative Reaction/Attitude   **Positive Reaction/Attitude**

SCENARIO TWO

A co-worker has just popped into your office 15 minutes before quitting time and asked you if you can give her a lift home. She lives 30 minutes from your home, and it will mean that you'll get home an hour late. However, you don't have any plans for the evening.

How do you react?

Negative Reaction/Attitude   **Positive Reaction/Attitude**

■ **WORKSHEET 4.1 (CONTINUED)**
Alter Your Attitude

SCENARIO THREE

Your boss has just notified you and some of your co-workers that the company is downsizing and you will be laid off in 30 days. He offers you a two-month severance package and tells you that the company will allow you to take time off during the 30 days to go on interviews as needed. You are completely surprised by this layoff, and all of your co-workers are very upset. Everyone is talking about how awful the company is and how terrible your boss is.

How do you react?

Negative Reaction/Attitude   **Positive Reaction/Attitude**

SCENARIO FOUR

You're 30-something and have a bachelor's degree in marketing. You've been working at this company for five years in a middle management position, hoping to get promoted to director of marketing. One day, the company president knocks on your door and brings in a 25-year-old woman who just obtained her MBA from Vanderbilt University. The president informs you that this woman is going to be your boss.

How do you react?

Negative Reaction/Attitude   **Positive Reaction/Attitude**

■ **WORKSHEET 4.1 (CONTINUED)**
Alter Your Attitude

Your goal should be to always hold others in the highest regard, to accept their strengths and weaknesses. Think the worst about people and they will give you their worst. Look for the highest good in people, and you will be surprised to see them living up to those high expectations. They will put their best foot forward. As others put their best foot forward, you will be more likely to put your best foot forward, too.

By giving of yourself and your time to others, you are saying, "You are worth my time. You are worth this moment." This is an example of thinking the best of others. Passing on this gift of the heart to others creates a bond between people—a bond of caring and goodwill. Give with your whole heart and soul.

HEART & SOUL TIP

Your goal should be to always hold others in the highest regard, to accept their strengths and weaknesses.

One caveat to all of this: Be aware that always thinking the best of others doesn't mean that you should let them walk all over you. Another important goal you should set is to trust your instincts to know when to draw the line and say, "This person is so negative, he's pulling me down. I need to stay away from him." Use your common sense to assess the situation. If someone is treating you in a bad way, you have to set boundaries and not let it affect your own self-esteem and self-worth.

While it's always best to look for the highest good in people, it's also realistic to be sensible when it comes to people who do you harm or who want to do you harm. If you're neutral in your thoughts toward them and stay away from those kinds of people, you can help turn negative stress into something positive.

Following are some examples to show you how to put your best thinking forward when dealing with others.

Thinking the Worst About Others	Thinking the Best About Others
She said she would call me this afternoon and we'd discuss my chances for promotion. I'll bet she won't call.	She said she would call this afternoon, and I'm sure she will if she has the time.
I would invite Sally to my after-work party, but she is such a loudmouth. I hate the way she dominates the conversation.	I will invite Sally to the party. She always has something to say and is great at entertaining people.
If we invite Jane, she'll bring her rowdy children. They'll probably tear up the house. I'll have to put everything out of reach, and that will be a hassle.	Jane is my friend and it's OK if she wants to bring her children over. They're such bright and energetic kids. I'll just put some stuff out of their reach before they arrive.
My parents treated me badly when I was a child. They yelled at me and never gave me the opportunities that children have today. It's their fault that I'm not as successful as others.	My parents did the best they knew how when they raised me. They gave me what they thought was necessary and did their best. It's up to me to find success, not my parents.

■ **TABLE 4.2**
Put Your Best Thinking Forward

Get the picture? When you're thinking the best about others, remember it also means that you're not jealous of others' good fortune. Being jealous or envious of others is another factor that contributes to negative stress. When you're thinking the best about people, you're also thinking happy thoughts for them. Be happy for others' good fortunes. Don't let resentfulness and jealousy take over your attitude, mood, and feelings.

When life is rough and you're having a hard time maintaining that positive attitude, continue to think the best about others. They will more than likely surprise you by treating you in the best way. And that alone will help to change that stress into positive energy.

Turn Mistakes into Opportunities

Making mistakes in life, and especially in your career, can cause stress. If something you do causes some sort of backlash—and it's the type of thing you'd rather not deal with—you're going to say, "I made a huge mistake." It's OK to say that, but, more important, what are you going to do about it? You want to take that mistake and turn it into an opportunity, as we've discussed throughout this chapter.

Bernie S. Siegel, author of *Prescriptions for Living,* as well as of *Love, Medicine, and Miracles* and *Peace, Love, and Healing,* states, "Mistakes are golden opportunities to show that you have heart."

Following is an example of how one man turned his on-the-job mistake into just such a golden opportunity.

CAREER
SUCCESS
STORY

Joe Bergman

Joe, a contractor, was hired to pave a driveway in a neighborhood in which he had never worked before. He went to the house and paved the driveway as scheduled. When he was finished, he knocked on the door to ask for payment. A woman he had never met before answered the door, and, after a few moments of confusion, Joe realized he had paved the wrong driveway.

The woman said that the driveway had needed paving anyway, so she offered to pay him something. However, Joe refused payment because he had made a mistake. "It's my mistake," he said, "so you owe me nothing." He told her that he had simply misread the address and apologized for his mistake. He moved his equipment to the home next door and proceeded to pave the correct driveway.

When the neighbors heard what Joe had done, they all began to talk about how nice this man was. Everyone in the neighborhood who needed a new driveway hired Joe, and he had more business than ever before—all because of his mistake on the job and the kindness he had shown, and because he showed that he had a good heart.

HEART & SOUL TIP

Mistakes are opportunities turned upside down.

This experience gave the woman a new "free" driveway and gave the kind contractor more business. Good hearts attract good hearts. Mistakes can be golden opportunities in disguise.

Instead of being stressed out that you made a huge mistake, you can offer kindness and a heartfelt attitude toward the situation, especially toward the person you "wronged" or affected with your mistake.

HEART & SOUL TIP

If you make a mistake, you always have another chance to make a fresh start any moment you choose. Failure is not falling down but staying down.

Many of us make mistakes in our careers and in our work. Knowing that you can use a mistake as an opportunity makes all the difference in the world. Often people think they messed up their lives with the careless decisions they made early in their careers. But that's not true. You really can't mess up your whole life—not if you realize that you're at the right place for you and your development, doing the right thing, no matter what it is.

HEART & SOUL TIP

Every experience in life and in our careers is designed to help us grow intellectually, mentally, physically, and spiritually.

We can all look back and think, "What if I had chosen that job? Or that profession?" Sure, it would have led us down a different road. But for whatever reason, you didn't choose that other job or career. You chose the one you're in right now, or the one you're planning on venturing into. Whatever decisions we make, we eventually work through the maze, intertwining our careers and personal lives the best we can. In other words, we are where we're supposed to be, even though it may be difficult and not the most wonderful situation in the world. Every experience in life and in our careers is designed to help us grow intellectually, mentally, physically, and spiritually. That's the synergistic Heart & Soul way and the only true, honest approach to life.

It often takes adversity to show you that your old methods of dealing with life are no longer appropriate. It's at these times that you need to develop new ways of responding, new ways to turn stress into an avenue for success. If you're used to getting angry when something happens that you don't like, it's

HEART & SOUL TIP

It often takes adversity to show you that your old methods of dealing with life are no longer appropriate.

time to change. If you're used to thinking negative thoughts about others, it's time to stop. If you're used to seeing your mistakes as the big problems and the reasons why you can't succeed in your career and in life, you should HALT right in your footsteps. If you blame everyone else for your own life and situation, stop now!

Take control of your life, your career, your situation, and make it a GREAT thing—a golden opportunity for growth and happiness.

In her book *You Can Heal Your Life*, Louise Hay states that the Law of Experience is always perfect and every experience is a success. There are no failures. She believes it's our natural birthright to go from success to success all our life. Each experience happens for a reason, and there's a lesson to be learned in each one. If we're not learning the lesson and not achieving success after success throughout our lives, then either we're not in tune with our inner selves, with our "highest" selves, or we don't believe it can be true for us. Many people have no faith in their ability to succeed and don't recognize their successes as they happen. How sad to not even recognize how wonderful and successful you are!

We recognize that life is hard, the career world is difficult, and, sure, it's harder for some than for others, but it's possible to survive tough situations in our careers and in our lives. Take this one step further and turn those tough situations into advantageous situations, into opportunities—golden opportunities. Take that tough situation and become someone who knows how to deal with life's tough problems.

Act as if you are the person you have always wanted to be. By acting like that person, you become that person. So, who do you want to be?

Accept Criticism

Criticism might sound like a major contributor to stress. But it's not, even though some people let it become a negative stress factor. Criticism can be a good thing and, if accepted in the right way, it can actually help you. If someone criticizes you, it means that people know you care about them and are willing to change. If no one criticizes you, that's a sign that people believe you don't care enough to listen and are not willing to change.

Think about your career up to this point. How many times have you been offered suggestions or critiques to improve your work or your career search? How many times have you listened and accepted criticism? Using this criticism in a positive way lightens your stress load. People are always offering us suggestions about how we can improve our services at the Heart & Soul Career Center. That's because they know we care and want to do our best for them. They've helped us fine-tune our services over the years and become better. We've listened to what their needs are and to their suggestions as to how we can help. If we hadn't listened, we'd still be a small company with no growth.

Bernie Siegel, in an article for *Family Circle* magazine, said that throughout his life and career he has had many good critics. Nurses handed him lists of ways he could improve, with practical suggestions such as using the intercom instead of bellowing out loud when he needed something. Patients gave him many good suggestions, too. They asked him to stop frightening them with his serious look and to smile when he entered their rooms. His family even helped him. Whenever he became demanding at home, they told him, "You're not in the operating room now."

The Sufi poet Rumi wrote, "Your criticism polishes my mirror." This means that criticism helps you focus on yourself better; it helps you see yourself more clearly. If you understand who you are and respect yourself, you will see criticism not as a problem but as an opportunity to become a better person. Siegel suggested that people respond with, "I'm sorry," and "Thank you for polishing my mirror." Almost always you can learn from the criticism and improve your behavior.

Of course, it's up to you to discern whether someone is criticizing you as a way to make himself or herself look and feel better. Unfortunately, some people love to find fault in others and don't know how to do anything but criticize. That's *their* problem, not yours. Don't let them force you to get stressed out in a negative way.

Accept Change

Some people really stress out over change. Most people don't like to change, even when it's "for the best." Any kind of change—especially career change—is a top stress-inducer in our lives and definitely a part of a Heart & Soul career tune-up. We become comfortable in situations—in our jobs, in our personal relationships—and even though we may be miserable, we don't like to change. Change is scary. It's the unknown.

But it doesn't have to be that way. You have a choice. You can view change as an exciting, positive adventure. Again, you have to concentrate on your attitude, your mood, and your feelings toward the change. If you view it as an adventure rather than a scary, unknown experience, your stress will be used in a positive rather than a negative way.

**CAREER
SUCCESS
STORY**

Jacob Michaels

Jacob Michaels came to see us because he was being promoted and transferred to Toronto, Ontario. He didn't want to go. He preferred to stay in Nashville, where he had grown up. As a result of this change, Jacob was stressing out in a negative way. He was willing to give up everything he had worked so hard for in his company—all because he didn't want to move to Toronto, because he didn't want to change.

We set up several career counseling sessions with him to help him reevaluate his career goals and strategies. We learned that he really did love his job in marketing and that this transfer would be a great boon to his career. The company had even promised him that, after a couple of years in Toronto, he probably could be transferred back to Nashville to head up a marketing venture there.

We advised Jacob, who was single and 28 years old, that he might want to view the transfer as a golden opportunity rather than a change for the worse.

HEART & SOUL TIP

Sometimes if you don't agree to change, you may miss out on a golden opportunity!

We focused on the positives of Toronto. "Just think," we told him, "about the multicultural environment, the new experiences and all those different restaurants! Think about all the museums and the different businesses in Toronto. Think about what you can learn by living in Toronto for two years!"

After several counseling and career-planning sessions, Jacob finally agreed to go. If he didn't take this transfer, he would lose a job he loved as well as an opportunity to experience another city. He would always have the option of returning to Nashville if he wanted to. He really had nothing to lose by going and everything to lose by staying!

Jacob accepted the transfer and moved to Toronto. He called three months later to thank us and to let us know that he loved Toronto. He wasn't even sure he ever wanted to move back to Nashville. "If you hadn't counseled me on the positive aspects of this career change, I wouldn't be here today," he told us.

Jacob accepted the change and used his stressful energy in a positive way. By accepting this career change and by switching his attitude to one of positivity instead of negativity, he succeeded.

Slow Down . . . Whoa . . . Stop there!

Slow down. We urge you to consciously make yourself stop and look around. Do you notice that the sky is a periwinkle color today—bits of purple and blue smudged into a beautiful panoramic umbrella? Can you smell the dewy cleanliness of the air? The freshly cut lawn? Those roses by the fence? Taking a moment to slow down each day can greatly affect your life. If you slow down, you can more easily manage your stress and turn it into positive energy.

HEART & SOUL TIP

You are in control of your life, and you can change how you use stress.

Most of us believe that we must "hurry, hurry, hurry" at all times—that we're not doing enough, not accomplishing enough. Please stop! You're speeding up your stress level a million beats per second. Turn it down. Slow down enough to look objectively at your stress, and use that energy in a positive way.

Changing your attitude, viewing your problems as golden opportunities, opening your heart, choosing success over failure, knowing that all experiences are good life experiences and life successes, seeing the highest good in others, accepting criticism, and accepting change are all ways to use stress in a positive manner. All of these, when flipped over and viewed negatively, can contribute to negative stress. You are in control of your life and you can change how you use stress. Whether it's a problem with your career or with your personal life, you can use stress to your advantage and to achieve success.

Embrace your stress and make it your best energy. Use your difficulties as opportunities. See the difference your attitude can make in your life. As Dan Millman writes in the book *Way of the Peaceful Warrior*, "We're all in training. Life can be difficult, but what an opportunity! Be guided by the best that's within you. It's said that there's one Journey but many paths. Here's wishing you well on your own path."

5 *Managing Negativity*

*Every good thought you think is contributing its
share to the ultimate result of your life.*

GRENVILLE KLEISER

O FAR, WE'VE EXPLORED how to embrace diversity more completely by utilizing Heart & Soul exercises and guidelines. We have introduced the Terrible Ten—the top 10 mistakes job seekers make. And we have dealt with learning how to use stress as a way to achieve success. Within all of these concepts lies a basic career and general life trap: the trap of *negativity*. We are born into this trap when we enter this life. We grow up in a basically negative world and we are programmed with negative thoughts from the day we are born.

In this chapter, we'll explore how to manage the negativity that's rampant in the workplace and in life! We'll examine how negative traps can jeopardize everything you've learned so far. We'll show you how to retrain yourself to be positive instead of negative and explore the benefits of a positive attitude. This is the fifth Heart & Soul secret of your Heart & Soul career tune-up.

Thoughts Are Real Things

You do know that thoughts are real things, don't you? A thought consists of a few micromilliwatts of real energy flowing through your brain—an almost unnoticed, unimportant event in your everyday process. How many times have you heard someone say, "I was only thinking about it. I didn't actually do it, so it doesn't count." Ah, but it *does* count. Your thoughts count. Even if you don't act on those thoughts, you've put out that energy and that energy is real.

Thoughts are powerful—overwhelmingly powerful, in fact. Our own thoughts have a significant impact on others, as well as on our own minds, bodies, and emotions. Thoughts can produce physical reactions in our bodies—

HEART & SOUL TIP

Thoughts are powerful and have a significant impact on others.

both good and bad. They influence our emotions. Think of something or someone you love. What do you feel? Now think of something or someone you despise. Feel the difference?

In this chapter, we'll show you how to change your thoughts and how this change will affect your emotions and attitudes. We'll show you how to manage negativity so that it doesn't enslave you and keep you hostage for the rest of your life.

Negative beliefs are exactly that: beliefs, not facts. Negative thoughts come to us from the media, our parents, our religion, our culture, our friends, and our associates. We are bombarded with negative thoughts, and this negativity shapes us, molds us, and makes us fearful, negative beings who cautiously walk through life, afraid to take chances, afraid to go after our dreams. When conducting a Heart & Soul career tune-up, it's vital that you address the negative issues in your life and learn how to manage them.

Because we live in a negative world, we can't avoid negative things. That's just not possible. But we can learn how to manage them and how to turn nega-

HEART & SOUL TIP

Negative beliefs are just that: beliefs, not facts.

tive thoughts into positive ones. We can learn how to live in the most positive, uplifting, and spiritual way possible.

When changing careers to find a job that's more in tune with your heart's goals and your life's mission, or when leaving a secure job for an uncertain future, it's probable that you'll be overwhelmed with negative thoughts such as the following.

I can't be successful doing what I love or want to do because

- I won't be able to find a job I love that pays what I need.
- I will hurt my family if I don't make enough money to support them in the way in which they're accustomed.
- I don't have very good ideas and do not know how to go about finding work that I love.
- It will upset my family if I leave this job and look for another.
- My friends will think I've gone crazy.

- I will think I've gone crazy.
- The world will think I've gone crazy.
- I will do bad work and end up looking like a fool.
- I will feel bad because I don't deserve to be successful doing something I love.
- It's too late for me. It's too late to change careers and succeed. I can't possibly start over in another career.
- I won't be able to handle the responsibility and will end up being self-destructive.
- I will die.

As you can see, this is the ultimate in negative thinking. This kind of thinking happens all the time when people want to change careers or are downsized in their jobs. It happens even when people are secure in a job because sometimes that security is only a shallow shield, hiding from them what they really want to do.

We let negative thoughts influence us and take over our lives. We let them imprison us so we cannot move. We let ourselves stagnate to the point of decay and destruction. It is necessary—vital to our very Heart & Soul existence—that we sweep away these negative thoughts.

If you find yourself in a negative space, remember that there's nothing wrong with you. You are not dumb, crazy, grandiose, silly, stupid, egomaniacal, or unrealistic just because you're unhappy and want to improve your life or get a job that is more in line with your dreams and goals. It is your birthright to do what you love in life. You are just afraid you won't succeed. Negative thinking can be sparked in all of us by many things, including the anger trap.

Managing the Anger Trap

Falling into an anger trap is easy. You are engulfed in negativity and it's very difficult to get out. The angrier you get, the deeper the negative abyss that you're drowning in. But it doesn't have to be this way. We can show you how to creatively use that anger in a positive way.

CAREER ROAD BLOCK STORY

Martin Shaw

Martin Shaw couldn't believe it. Only 37 years old, he had been working as a senior accountant for a large hospital in Boulder, Colorado, for eight years. He was good at his job and had been recognized as employee of the month several times. His supervisor, the controller, had turned in his resignation two months earlier and Martin wanted that job. He revised his resume and turned it in to the chief financial officer. He was quite sure he'd get the job; after all, he was next in line for promotion.

One morning Martin came in to work and was introduced to John Kelley—the new controller! Martin couldn't believe it. He was furious. How could they hire someone from the outside for that position when he was next in line?

He blew up. Without getting all the facts, he stormed into the CFO's office and said that he was quitting—that it wasn't fair for the hospital to hire a new controller from the outside and not promote him. He ranted and raved for a good 20 minutes. The CFO calmly told him fine and good luck. Martin, his face red, bolted out of the office that day, and six months would pass before he found another job. Because of his anger and lack of discipline, Martin put himself and his family through a very difficult period—with no money and few job prospects.

Unfortunately, little did Martin know, but the CFO had been planning to promote him to a senior controller's position. He would have been over the new controller and would have received a huge salary increase.

Martin should have gone to the CFO and clearly and calmly discussed his concern about being passed over for a promotion. If he had done this, the CFO would have told him he had nothing to worry about. Instead, Martin let his anger get the better of him, and as a result, he was out on the streets without a job for months.

HEART & SOUL TIP

Tuning up your career also means tuning up your emotions.

It's important that we discuss anger at this point because it is such a prominent part of people's lives and is displayed throughout the workplace and in all work environments. Tuning up your career means that you should also tune up emotions that can either help you or hinder you in your job.

Anger is a tremendous energy—a potent fuel that's boiling and boiling—a raw power, open-edged, jagged, and biting. It can tear you apart and completely destroy you if you're not aware in the moment and if you're not disciplined enough to handle it, which is what happened to Martin. Anger, when used in the wrong way, is negativity at its bleakest. It can be a reactive emotion that explodes like wildfire when not disciplined and tamed.

"There is no room for peace of mind or love in our hearts when the ego is telling us to value anger and hate. The moment we accept the belief that we are victims, fear and anger dominate our lives," states Gerald G. Jampolsky in *Out of the Darkness into the Light*.

Anger can destroy you, especially if you believe you are a victim. But there are no victims in life. We create our own situations and our own lives, so anger doesn't have to destroy us at all. We can use anger as a tool so that it works for us rather than against us. In her book *The Artist's Way*, Julia Cameron explains that "Anger is meant to be listened to. Anger is a voice, a shout, a plea, a demand. Anger is meant to be respected because it is a map."

When you have anger within you, there is power and direction. You can use this power as fuel to act. Anger shows you where you've been and lets you know when you haven't liked it. But it can be a sign of health, too. It can be the impetus that moves you to where you need to be. For example, when you

HEART & SOUL TIP

If you use your anger constructively, it can be a powerful, effective tool.

see someone living the kind of life you want to live, you might react like this: "Darn it! I could do that better than she can. Why can't I get that kind of job? I have just as many skills and talents!"

This is anger's voice saying, "OK, if you think that you can do it better and that you have just as many skills and talents, then get going!" This anger is telling you that it's time to change your life. If you use your anger constructively, it can be a powerful, effective tool. Anger can be your friend—a potent friend that makes you sit up and take notice of your life and your career. It can make you act in your own best interest.

There are two kinds of anger that can be very destructive: the kind that's hidden deep within and the kind that is explosive and reactive to an outer force. But you can funnel your anger into a positive force if you use its power to motivate you in positive ways.

Fueling Depression

Anger that's hidden deep within becomes depression, and depression is a form of negativity. You might look at depression as something that attacks you from time to time—out of nowhere—that's just a result of lots of rain and gray skies. But depression is more than this. (Of course, we're not talking about clinical depression. That's a physiological problem and isn't the same as emotional depression.)

Emotional depression is a result of subdued, repressed anger and negative feelings and is often accompanied by a sense of tiredness and helplessness. One of the reasons people are so often tired and depressed is that we have become pros at negativity—at hiding our anger, our hurts, our fears, and our wants and needs.

When you hide your true feelings on an ongoing basis, you can become a martyr, a whiner, or a complainer. Or perhaps you might distract yourself from your problems with drugs, alcohol, or food.

HEART & SOUL TIP

The moment you stop pretending that everything is OK, your healing begins. Your energy will start to flow again and your negativity and depression will dissipate.

Some people are so used to hiding their anger that they don't recognize it anymore. They may not even notice that they're angry. If you can admit your anger—the anger that's hidden deep within—and if you can tell someone what's bothering you, or at least acknowledge it to yourself, you can diffuse the anger and get rid of it. It's best to uncover hidden feelings of anger and deal with them. Otherwise, you'll become tired and depressed.

We all have a tendency to avoid certain feelings at times. We may try to avoid confrontations and unpleasant situations. But if you can tune in to your inner self and understand your feelings, you can handle the negative side effects. Admit it if you're hurt or angry, and start to turn your feelings around.

Sometimes people think of themselves as victims when they experience hurt or angry feelings—as in Martin's case. He thought he was a victim of unfairness in his workplace. He didn't stop and think before he lost his temper. It's imperative for you to avoid thinking of yourself as a victim and, equally important, to avoid placing the blame on other people or things. Once you start taking full responsibility for your life, your life will change. You will be on the road to being in charge of your life and your destiny, and depression will be a thing of the past.

Whenever you start feeling sorry for yourself and thinking of yourself as a victim in a relationship or in any other situation, force yourself to start thinking as the master of your own life. You own your life; no one else does. You own each moment, each hour, each day of your life.

HEART & SOUL TIP

There are no victims in life. We are all responsible for our acions and our conditions.

Many times in a personal or even a career/professional relationship, we find ourselves playing one of three roles: the victim, the persecutor, or the rescuer. Recognize any of these? Each of these roles can be deadly, so be forewarned. They can all lead to depression and to negativity in our lives. If you engage in these types of relationships, whether business or personal, your problems are going to get worse. It is most difficult to solve your problems if you're playing one of these roles in a personal or career relationship.

Look around you at this moment to identify people, situations, or things that tend to make you feel like a victim: undesirable mate, undesirable job, controlling friends or family—all of these factors can work to make you feel like a victim.

The persecutor role is closely related to that of victim. If you find yourself playing the victim or the persecutor, you'll recognize yourself here. Do you perceive yourself as the victim of your spouse, your boss, or the world? Do you persecute everyone around you because you're unhappy in your present

HEART & SOUL TIP

You're responsible for your life being the way it is. As soon as you realize this, you gain the power to create the life you want.

situation? These negative attitudes are eating up your creative energy. You can use this victim energy—or this "persecution" energy—to change your life. Take charge and be responsible for your situation. You do not have to be a victim or a persecutor and you do not have to be depressed. You simply do not have to live with negative thoughts.

It's not a good idea to be around people who also see you as a victim. These people support your sense of weakness and delay your progress toward taking full control of your life.

Being in the role of the rescuer is also toxic to your overall health. A person who comes to your rescue during your times of feeling like a victim is strengthening your victim role. For example, let's say you call a friend and say, "My boss told me that my ideas were stupid. I can't believe he treated me that way." Your friend responds, "He obviously doesn't respect you. You're going nowhere in this job." This response may seem compassionate, but look deeper. It's affirming that you are a victim and that you are weak, and it supports your belief that you're a loser. Don't set up your friends so that they relate to you as a victim. And do the same for them. Support one another, and remind one another in a loving way that each of you is responsible for your life being the way it is. As soon as you realize this, you gain the power to create the life you want.

Seek out friends who help you out of your victim feelings. A friend is a person who reminds you that you are unique, special, and worthy. A friend is someone who reminds you that you hold immense power, divine power, that you can use to achieve what you want in your career and life. The moment you take full responsibility for your life and career, the depression—the negative cocoon you find yourself in—will begin to dissolve.

Using Affirmations to Fight Negativity

Affirmations can serve as a tool to help you in your battle against negativity. An affirmation is a positive belief about yourself; there are many ways to use affirmations to chase away negativity. The positive power of self-affirmations can change your life.

HEART & SOUL TIP

The positive power of self-affirmations can change your life.

Most successful people have used affirmations to succeed. Scott Adams, the creator of the popular "Dilbert" cartoon strip, said he always visualized himself as the nation's top cartoonist. He figured out that to live big dreams you must first visualize them. While working as a middle manager at a communications company, he would write, "I will be a syndicated cartoonist" 15 times a day. This positive affirmation worked. Later, Adams decided he wanted to have the top comic strip, so he visualized the retirement of Gary Larson ("The Far Side") and Bill Watterson ("Calvin and Hobbes"). And it happened.

If Scott had said, "Oh, I'll never be a top cartoonist because there are so many other great cartoonists out there," he never would have succeeded. If he had said, "Oh, there's no way I can leave my day job and be successful doing what I love most," Scott would still be a middle manager. Instead of letting negative thoughts keep him in a position he didn't enjoy, he used creative thoughts and affirmations to obtain the kind of life he wanted—a life doing what he loved most.

HEART & SOUL TIP

Our mind is simply an intellectual box that reflects what we put into it.

Our mind is simply an intellectual box that reflects what we put into it. It's programmable and that's why it's so easy to stay in a negative mode. If your mind continually hears negative comments, you begin to think negatively—by habit. If the mind "hears" that you're not worthy of that better job, it begins to "believe" it.

CAREER SUCCESS STORY

Fabienne Cousteau

Fabienne Cousteau was from France. She moved to the United States a few years ago and settled in New York City. "I want to find a job in interior design," she told us, "but my background is in project management for import/export businesses and I don't believe any interior design firm will hire me."

She didn't have any experience in interior design, and she believed this meant that she'd never find a job with a design firm, even though she loved working on interiors.

We counseled Fabienne for two months. We discovered that she did indeed have the skills and qualifications needed for this kind of job. She had been redecorating friends' homes and offices for years! Plus, she was dynamite in client relations and customer service—two crucial areas that all interior designers need.

We told Fabienne that she needed to change her attitude. We helped her develop a list of positive affirmations and told her to write them down 15 times a day.

HEART & SOUL TIP

If you keep believing what you've been believing, then you'll keep achieving what you've been achieving. If you keep getting what you're getting, it's because you keep doing what you're doing.

Here's one of Fabienne's affirmations:

"I have many good talents and qualifications to offer an interior design firm. I am employed at one of the top interior design firms in New York City and I am happy."

Every day, Fabienne repeated this affirmation 15 times while looking in the mirror. And we told her to always act "As if." By acting "As if" you have already achieved your goal, you are already manifesting the change and bringing it into reality. By writing down this affirmation, by acting "As if" and repeating the affirmation aloud to herself in the mirror, Fabienne was retraining her mind to think positively instead of negatively. The more she repeated the affirmation, the more her mind believed it.

We rewrote her resume and marketing materials to help her focus on a job in interior design. We focused on her creative talents and all her informal experience as an interior designer. Within two months, Fabienne called us and said, "It's amazing how these affirmations have worked in my life. I have been offered two jobs in interior design firms, and it's because I trained myself to believe I could do it!"

Remember, you have the power to change your thoughts. If you believe that negative things will happen in your life, negative things *will* keep happening. If you keep getting things that are not good, it's because you keep doing the same negative things in your life to bring these things to you.

Retrain yourself as Fabienne did. Write down a positive affirmation 15 times a day and say it out loud while looking at yourself in the mirror. Before you know it, you'll achieve your goals—and a new attitude.

The following worksheet page is for you. Use this page to write down your own affirmations. Within a few days you'll begin to notice a change in your attitude. We promise you that if you are persistent with this exercise, you will get results.

POSITIVE AFFIRMATIONS

1.

2.

3.

4.

5.

6.

7.

8.

9.

10.

11.

12.

13.

14.

15.

■ **WORKSHEET 5.1**
Create 15 Personal Affirmations

We assume that, if you're reading this book, you're in the process of becoming a Heart & Soul career tune-up scientist—a person who really wants to know, analyze, and understand yourself and your career decisions on an in-depth level. Because of this, you're not like the typical career person. You know there's a holistic approach to accomplishing everything and you want to utilize this approach in your career as well as in other parts of your life. That's why you're interested in knowing how to tune into your inner self, how to manage anger, and how to creatively master negativity during your Heart & Soul career tune-up.

Walk into Yourself

Maybe you've been too busy in your life to look inward on an in-depth level. Maybe you're at a point where life isn't very fulfilling. Whatever your reasons, you've decided to get to know yourself and your career aspirations on a Heart & Soul level. You're not satisfied with everyday answers to life's most intimate questions. You want to know who you are, why you're here, and how to establish a Heart & Soul career plan. You want to take your life to the next level. You need to *walk into yourself!*

Walking is a great tool for reawakening your connection with yourself. It is one of the most powerful and creative Heart & Soul tools. Walking is a type of meditation/contemplation exercise that can be a vital source of creativity. It provides a constant inflow of new images, thoughts, revelations, and feelings. It opens us to that great inner source of life where inspiration and creativity dwell. And it is very important when tuning up your career.

Walking is an ancient form for pursuing a life path—a vision quest. For more than 4,000 years, Aborigines, native Australians, have walked in Dreamtime—a timeless dimension during which they dream toward the future and the future dreams back. It is a way of linking up with spirit. It is in this timeless dimension that they connect with their inner selves. There are many books on shamanism that explore and explain Dreamtime at some length. Think of it as a channel of consciousness—a scientific band or wavelength where both time and events are flexible. In that realm, positive dreams take on reality.

In ancient times, Druids and Wiccans walked on long quests. Tibetans still make circular pilgrimages around Kalais, the sacred mountain that is Shiva's birthplace. Native Americans walk on vision quests.

Whenever any of us goes for a walk, we embark on an inner voyage as well as an outer voyage. Walking is a Heart & Soul exercise that will help you reconnect with who you are and what your career dreams are. During a walk, you can work on affecting and changing your career future by changing the way you think. You can plan that next career move or transition. All missions,

HEART & SOUL TIP

When you take your walks, go alone and pay attention to all the sounds and beauty around you

whether career goals or life's dreams, begin with a single thought. While you are walking, some of your thoughts may become your destiny.

As you walk, you can move your thinking to more positive possibilities. You begin to experience broader horizons and more expanded possibilities. That's why walking is an important tool to use when managing negativity and in all parts of your Heart & Soul career tune-up.

Block out 20 minutes a day and walk. The only rule is that you must walk by yourself, since walking with someone else will take your attention away from your own thoughts. You can take your walk any time during the day. Twilight is a favorite time for many people because it feels like a time between worlds—between day and night, a soft time with soft light and red-purple wine sunsets and deepening blue skies. It is a time when the world is yawning and stretching lazily before you, falling in soft blue whispers and pale moon shadows, a time when the world is getting ready to sleep, but it still light enough for you to observe and listen.

When you walk, pay attention to the Earth around you. Do you feel the cool wind blowing a breath of freshness on your face? Do you see the sunlight filtering gold dust through the leaves? Look at the speckles of gold topping the trees and swaying with the wind. And what about the sky? Have you ever

HEART & SOUL TIP

Adopting an "attitude of gratitude" on a regular basis will raise your state of consciousness and increase your ability to manage negativity.

seen such a crisp blue? Have you ever noticed how the tree branches crisscross in intricate designs and patterns? No wonder visual artists love trees. Take a deep breath and take in all of the world's loveliness. Be grateful for who you are and your life. Think of the things in life that you love—your mate, your family, your friends, your pets. This "attitude of gratitude" has been talked about by many spiritual leaders throughout the years. By being grateful for and reflecting on your life, you are actually viewing your life from a higher state of consciousness.

Adopting an attitude of gratitude on a regular basis will raise your state of consciousness and increase your ability to manage negativity and make better, wiser decisions. (We discuss this attitude of gratitude in depth in *Heart & Soul Resumes*.) It will also help you identify and embrace your inner Heart & Soul self, because the closer you get to knowing yourself, the closer you'll be to understanding the importance of your life.

The simple act of gratitude is powerful and can certainly change your life. It can affect every aspect of your day and can change your mood from negative

HEART & SOUL TIP

Listening is an important tool for overcoming anger traps and negative blockades.

to positive. The mystic Meister Eckhart was quoted as saying, "If the only prayer you say in your whole life is 'thank you' that would suffice."

While you're walking, listening can be another important tool for overcoming anger traps and negative blocks. You might think you're a good listener, but it's very likely that you're only half-listening most of the time. It takes training and practice to learn how to truly listen. You can start by listening to the sounds of life.

Walking is a Heart & Soul exercise in heightened listening. While you are walking, pay attention to the primal earth sounds around you. Do you hear life speaking to you? Do you hear the earth humming and vibrating? People who live in rural areas and who walk out in the woods and fields often report hearing the "sounds of life."

In a popular movie a few years ago titled *Flatliners,* starring Julia Roberts and Keifer Sutherland, young medical students would take themselves to the point of death and then bring themselves back to life. During that time they "flatlined" and were legally dead, and each experienced some kind of "out-of-body" adventure. After many "flatliners," Sutherland's character stated that he had learned there was a constant humming, a buzzing sound that permeated all of life. From this sound came all things.

In the late 1990s a television series called *Roar* aired briefly. Set in medieval times and featuring Druids and Celts, the show introduced a spiritual Master who explained that the "roar" was a constant humming sound that existed in all of life, and that when you were in total harmony with life, you could hear this sound.

The "sound of life" is a real sound you can hear on the inside. It is a humming vibration and usually sounds like an audio tone that comes from a TV or radio. This "life sound" can be heard differently, too. Some people report that it sounds like a group of buzzing bees, or a waterfall. Some have said that late at night when they are in bed or are alone they can hear the melodic sound of a flute. If you hear one of these sounds, you can be assured that you're connecting with the Life Source. These are all sounds that connect you with your inner self and help you understand who you are on a Heart & Soul level.

Tom Brown

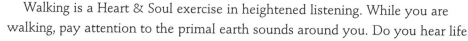

CAREER SUCCESS STORY

Tom Brown lived in the Midwest and ran a dairy farm. His career goal was to have a successful dairy farm and be able to live an independent life—free from corporate bureaucracy. As with any career or business, the farm often had problems, and Tom would lapse into hours of negativity and self-doubt. His bills far exceeded his profits. He worried that he might have to file for bankruptcy—or worse, sell the farm.

Because of his troubles, Tom experienced feelings of self-pity, negativity, and anger. He lashed out at everyone. When he came to us for career counseling, we suggested that he learn how to manage his negativity, his anger, and his attitude before tackling anything else. "As in any career tune-up," we told him, "you have to take care of your inner problems before you can succeed with the outer ones." We advised him to start meditating. For Tom, walking was the best way to practice meditation. It offered him a natural way to meditate and get in touch with his inner heart and soul.

Struggling to understand his problems and wishing he could overcome them, Tom began to spend many hours meditating while walking out in the fields of clover and golden wheat. Then one morning he experienced something unusual. He couln't figure it out.

Tom told us that, all of a sudden, when he went out into the pastures early in the morning to gather his cows for milking and to do his meditations, he began to hear heavenly music. This music scared him, but it also soothed and comforted him. It was unlike any sound or music he had ever heard before.

Tom had to get up every day at 3:00 A.M. to gather his cows to the barn for milking. The early morning was always pitch black with only a glimmer of twinkling stars and a pale moon overhead. Tom had discovered that it was an excellent time to do meditations because the earth was so quiet and still. His dog, Sam, a brown and white collie, trotted quietly alongside him. There were no sounds, no voices anywhere—no cars, no horns, no chitter-chatter of people. It was just Tom and his dog and the world. Tom said it wasn't long before every morning, as regular as the dawning of the day itself, he could hear this beautiful music coming from the ethers, out of nowhere. It was a mystery to Tom and his family.

"It sounded like flutes and organs," Tom said. "I figured it must be church music from one of the Boy Scout camps in the area." However, after checking with those camps, Brown discovered that none of them played church music at

3:00 A.M. In fact, they all denied playing music at all! Finally, Tom concluded that he was hearing the music of life—that somehow it would help him, and it did. Tom told us that the music washed the negativity away, that instead he found himself smiling, whistling, and feeling optimistic about life. The music—the sound of life—lifted him out of his despair and negativity. As a result, Tom took a more active approach to paying his bills, getting out of debt, and increasing his profits from his farm and dairy cattle. By tuning into his inner self, by walking and listening to life's sounds, Tom found an inner peace and happiness that's often hard to find in today's career world.

Even today, Tom says that any time he goes out into the fields early in the morning before the world is awake, he can still hear this heavenly sound. "That sound completely changed my thinking," he explained. "Whenever I heard it I couldn't be negative. I felt happy. As a result, my farm business grew more and more as I became more positive when dealing with folks."

Many people can tune into this life sound on a daily basis. You can, too, with some practice. We recommend trying to "tune into" this sound while you walk or during a spiritual exercise or meditation. Believe it or not, tuning into this sound can help you in your everyday experiences at work, just as it helped Tom on his farm. It is a wonderful tool for managing negativity and stress.

Perhaps you live in a hectic, noisy city. Forests and parks are often the best places for meditative walking, but you can find good paths even if you live in the city—be it quiet back streets or parks. Try walking in the evening twilight, when most people are sitting down to eat. Or wait until after dinner, when it is almost dark.

If you can't find a quiet place outside, you might listen to your radio and try walking to music. Some people like to listen to their favorite music while walking. With the right music caressing your spirit, you can walk right past boisterous construction sites, noisy people, barking dogs, and screeching tires, without any of them bothering you! You can "see" beyond of all of this. You can see inside yourself. It doesn't really matter what time of the day you do your walking. What matters is that you do it. Walking moves us into intimacy with ourselves. Music is another way to open your awareness. For example, in recent years, Gregorian chants, Native American drum music, and other rhythmic types of music have become quite popular. This kind of sacred music can open your heart and help you tune into your inner self.

HEART & SOUL TIP

Music is a wonderful tool for managing negativity, and it can help transport you into other worlds and completely erase the negativity of the day.

Music can take you places. It can lift you from the humdrum of life and transport you into other worlds. It can open your heart and completely erase the negativity of the day. After all, music is a sound of life, too. Many people listen to music in their offices throughout the day. It's a great Heart & Soul tool for managing negativity.

HEART & SOUL TIP

When you walk into the outer world, you are moving consciously into your inner world.

Walking will bring you many gifts. You'll find answers to problems that have been plaguing you. You'll be inspired with new ideas and thoughts. You'll automatically erase negative thoughts and replace them with productive, positive thoughts and feelings. When you walk into the outer world, you are moving consciously into your inner world. You are actually moving with the "flow of life."

Self-Talk

Along with walking and listening to the life sounds within and around you, including music, during your Heart & Soul career tune-up, we believe it's vital to pay attention to what you say when you engage in "inner" talk. In *What to Say When You Talk to Your Self,* author Shad Helmstetter writes that it's important to replace old self-talk (negative thinking) with positive new self-talk. Helmstetter writes, "By replacing your earlier negative or neutral self-talk with new commands, you are activating healthy, productive chemical and electrical control centers in your brain which will automatically work for you instead of against you."

HEART & SOUL TIP

Inner talk is important to practice when you want to replace negative thoughts with positive ones.

Dr. Norman Vincent Peale, in his book *The Power of Positive Thinking,* discusses many ways to help people readjust their thinking and do better in their lives. Most people will agree that you should think positive thoughts at all times, that negative thoughts are not good for you. But it's one thing to think positive and another to act positive. If you don't retrain yourself with positive affirmations and self-talk, you won't be successful at maintaining a positive attitude in life. Positive thinking is only temporary if you don't reprogram your mind. That's why it's important to know what to say when you talk to yourself.

The trick is to replace your negative thoughts with new positive ones and to routinely say these aloud to yourself over and over. The purpose is to push out all those negative thoughts. An example of this is shown in Table 5.2.

Most of us are not even aware that we constantly feed ourselves with negative thoughts. We are not aware that we have a constant internal dialogue that sends us messages. We often don't pay attention to the internal dialogue that plays like a broken record in our minds.

If you pay attention to this internal dialogue and replace those negative thoughts with positive statements, you can change your life and embark on a path to success. Remember, anything that you say out loud to yourself, or even to someone else about yourself or about anything else, can be part of your self-talk, your personal affirmation. Everything you say when speaking out loud or thinking to yourself will give your mind information. So, make this information positive information. Retrain yourself and soon you will be a person that you can truly like and admire.

Thoughts are things. Positive thoughts like joy, happiness, fulfillment, success, achievement, worthiness, calm, enthusiasm, well-being, energy, ease, and love have positive results. Negative thoughts such as judgments, unworthiness,

HEART & SOUL TIP

If you don't retrain yourself with positive affirmations and self-talk, you won't be successful at maintaining a positive attitude in life.

HEART & SOUL TIP

Anything you say out loud to yourself or to someone else, about yourself or about anything else, is part of your self-talk, your personal affirmation.

Old Negative Thought	New Positive, Affirming Thought
I can't	I *can*
He won't like me	*Of course* he'll like me
I don't deserve	I *do* deserve
I won't succeed	I *can* succeed
I can't find a job	I *am* finding a great job
I am a failure	I *am* successful
I am ugly	I *am* beautiful
I am tired	I possess *all the energy I need*
I don't have time for this	I *have* time to do what I need

■ **TABLE 5.2**
Replacing Negative Thoughts with Positive Thoughts

hate, mistrust, resentment, fear, anxiety, tension, alienation, and anger all have negative results.

HEART & SOUL TIP

Thoughts are real things. Make yours positive and worthwhile.

Remember, you don't have to stay negative. You don't have to let anger control your life. You are in control of yourself. Change yourself for the better. Change your heart if you need to. But by all means, enjoy your life. Enjoy the heart and soul of your existence. Walk . . . listen . . . know . . . understand . . . dream. Enjoy all of life. It is a wonderful gift, and it is such a waste of energy and time to keep yourself in the clutches of negativity.

Mastering Change

Here is what is truly amazing about life.
Things change.

ELIZABETH GLASER

AT SOME POINT IN your career, you'll probably find yourself going through a dramatic change. Either you'll be "downsized," "right-sized," or transferred, or you'll outgrow your current position and find yourself yearning for something better. Or you'll go through a complete career transition. No matter what it is, change can be unsettling and stressful, but at the same time, it can be very exciting and inspiring.

It's important to remember that everything is subject to change. Nothing ever really stays the same. At any given moment life can throw us a dollop of changes in health, career, finances, relationships, and even our own spirituality. Many people don't know how to handle change, let alone master it. At best, they muddle through a change, often bitter and resentful, and often complaining about it. But, just as you don't have to let stress overwhelm your life with negativity, neither do you have to let change affect you in a negative way. It's important to recognize that change can be an opportunity to make your life and career better and more spiritually fulfilling.

In this chapter, we'll explore ways to create and manifest change and to use this change as a springboard to creating a better career and life. Our methods will help you during your Heart & Soul career tune-up. Whether you're staying in the same job or moving on to something else, you can learn how to master change. This is our sixth secret to capturing heart and soul in your work life. We believe it's a crucial part of any Heart & Soul career tune-up.

Change can come at any time in your career and life. It can be a planned event or a surprise event. It can be a slow process or a fast one. Of course, planned changes can be easier than those that are unplanned, but change is change no matter how it happens.

HEART & SOUL TIP

Change can come at any time in your career and life. Just as you don't have to let stress overwhelm your life with negativity, neither do you have to let change affect you in a negative way.

Making Planned Changes (Goal Setting)

Some people consciously create goals and work toward achieving them in the process of creating change. Once they achieve their goals, the complete change occurs. We must continue to make changes in our lives and careers if we want to grow. If we don't make changes, we become stagnant and dull. Change is about growth. About development. About becoming better mentally, physically, and spiritually. The process of setting goals and achieving them will bring about change. It's important to dream and to establish goals to fulfill those dreams, and it's important to know how to implement any changes in your life once those dreams manifest.

A true Heart & Soul change is about incorporating a synergistic approach toward life. Setting goals will help you accomplish any change, whether it's in your career or in your personal life.

HEART & SOUL TIP

Setting goals will help you accomplish change, whether it's in your career or in your personal life.

In Mary Carroll Moore's book *How to Master Change in Your Life,* Moore writes about the three essential elements that help us set successful goals that will grow as we grow. They are (1) an awareness that life, God, the Higher Power, helps you reach your goals, (2) an understanding that the goals that really satisfy are those that fulfill your purpose in life, and (3) the constant inner listening that allows you to adjust your goals to match your growth.

We often set goals, but, along the way, we can experience problems. We may see these problems as our own failures. We lose faith in our goals and in our ability to succeed. But problems don't mean that you or your goal are flawed. And if you don't reach your goals, you can think of it as an opportunity to reevaluate them and set new ones. Reevaluating your goals is an opportunity to match your goals to your own spiritual and intellectual growth.

As we mentioned previously, failure can be an opportunity to try again and try differently. Do you think any scientist ever succeeds on the first try or any

Olympic champion wins a medal on his or her first try? Of course not! Likewise, you should not expect that you'll always achieve your goals the first time. Look at your failures as practice—and remember that practice makes perfect. The more you practice (or fail), the more skilled you'll become, and ultimately, you will achieve your goal.

HEART & SOUL TIP

The best goals in life and in your career bring you the opportunities that help you to be a better individual personally as well as more successful career person.

The best goals in life and in your career bring you the opportunities that help you to be a better individual personally, as well as a more successful career person. They bring out the best in you. If you're in tune with your inner self—if you're meditating and listening to your inner voice—you're more than likely on the right track in your life, and you'll reach your goals.

Following is an example of how two of our clients used goal setting and change to improve their lives, even though the outcome wasn't exactly what they had planned.

Chandler and Roxanne Harmon

CAREER SUCCESS STORY

Chandler and Roxanne came to our office looking despairing. Chandler had been a top sales executive with a television station in Los Angeles, and Roxanne had been equally successful as a talent scout for a large film production company. They both had become disillusioned with Los Angeles—riots, pollution, and sky-high home prices. So, about two years ago, they wrote a list of goals:

- Move to a smaller city with less traffic congestion, no riots, and more reasonable home prices.
- Find a job for Chandler in a small company that offers more operational control and decision making with opportunities for growth and partnership. This job should allow Chandler the ability to serve others and to "make a real difference in people's lives."
- Find a job for Roxanne that nurtures her creativity and allows her to explore spiritual principles more freely.

It took two years for these goals to manifest. Through a headhunter, Chandler was contacted by a new company in Nashville that wanted him to develop an entire sales department for a new television station. He was offered a full partnership in the company and numerous incentives. It was his dream job. He could create his own policies for training salespeople. He could build and nurture their development and thus make a real difference in their lives, which was his "higher purpose."

After visiting Nashville, Roxanne and Chandler were certain that this was the place they wanted to move—no gangs, not as much traffic congestion, and reasonably priced housing. In addition, because of Nashville's thriving music industry, Roxanne was quite confident that she would be able to find a creative job in film or music production.

However, along with all of this goal setting and planning came fears. They were surprised at the fear that overcame them concerning their move to Nashville. Fear is a powerful force and one of the main reasons people don't succeed in achieving their goals and dreams. So, for a few months, Roxanne and Chandler put their lives on hold. They were afraid to make the move, even though it seemed like everything would be great. They were afraid of the change—the unknown. Los Angeles was comfortable, even though they were miserable there.

In *Ask the Master, Book 2,* Harold Klemp writes, "Each life cycle has a growth and fulfillment stage. We switch back and forth between them. The growth phase begins with a restless feeling that urges us into a new and greater opportunity, but fear holds us back. Finally, this need for growth outweighs the fear." Finally, Roxanne and Chandler's need for growth outweighed their fears and they decided to make the move.

Setting their goals and achieving them had forced them to change. And even though they were afraid of the change, they knew that they had to do it if they wanted to grow and develop their lives in a more harmonious, synergistic way that was compatible with their career dreams and desired lifestyle.

Although they planned this change and asked for it, it turned out to be more difficult than they had anticipated. They hadn't realized how fear would become an obstacle and how they would have to overcome that fear.

Roxanne and Chandler could have opted to let fear take control of their lives. They could have stayed in Los Angeles, but they knew they would have become stagnant and would not have fulfilled their dreams. You can always opt to back out of a change—that's the easy way. But sometimes life forces you to change whether you like it or not. How you handle or master that change is up to you.

Roxanne and Chandler overcame their fear, sold their home in Los Angeles, and moved to Nashville. The move was stressful, as any move is, but they managed the stress quite well, focusing their energy on getting organized and on their dreams of living in a more harmonious environment.

Once in Nashville, they settled into a routine and every week became just another week. But Chandler soon discovered that the new television station was poorly managed and might not even survive. And Roxanne had a difficult time finding a job. Both of them became quite disillusioned and disappointed with their move. After all, they had been very successful in Los Angeles and had earned a six-income figure, and now here they were, living in Tennessee and quite uncertain about their careers and future. With only one income, times were tough. They began to argue, blaming each other for their problems. Roxanne didn't like the humidity and Chandler didn't like the cold winters and the rain. They began to focus on all the negative things they could think of about Nashville. Things got worse and worse.

HEART & SOUL TIP

The best way to deal with change is to change yourself.

HEART & SOUL TIP

Even planned changes can be difficult and scary.

HEART & SOUL TIP

Sometimes life forces you to change whether you like it or not. How you handle or master that change is up to you.

When they came to see us, we set up individual career counseling sessions with each of them. We told them they needed to view this change in their lives in a positive way. They had to stop focusing on all the negative things and change their attitudes. They had to take charge of life and not let life take charge of them.

We rewrote their resumes to target the markets they were interested in. Then, we prepared a job search campaign and located companies that would be interested in their qualifications.

We showed them how to use the change in their lives in a positive way. "After all," we explained, "you have achieved your goals of moving to a smaller city where there's less traffic, no riots, and lower housing prices. Along with any change comes adjustment."

Rarely does something happen exactly as planned. Life doesn't always behave according to our rules. If we listen to our inner nudging and our inner guidance, though, we are more likely to be in sync with life's rules. Going with the flow will always ease your life considerably and will make each change a more pleasant one. So we worked with Chandler and Roxanne to help them adjust to the bumps they had encountered in this life change. We encouraged them to practice meditation exercises on a regular basis to stay tuned in to their inner guidance.

While meditating one morning, Chandler hit upon an idea: Why not find investors and buy the television station himself? He was surprised at this inner message, but he knew he had nothing to lose. So he used his creative ingenuity to find investors to buy the floundering television station and make him a partner. As a partner at the television station, Chandler was able to create a work environment that was aligned with his goals and dreams of making a real impact on people's lives.

Roxanne spent a lot of time meditating and searching her inner self for answers to her questions, too. After a while, she found a job as a personal assistant to a successful musician. Roxanne found work in a very creative environment and developed her talents and skills in the music industry.

Often, a crisis or even an illness can be a blessing in disguise. When Chandler discovered that the television station was about to go bankrupt, he first saw it as a crisis. But we helped him realize that this was an opportunity for growth instead of stress and uncertainty. After talking to several banks, he was able to solicit investors and save the television station from bankruptcy. Plus, he became a partner, which meant that he had decision-making power and a new avenue for career growth.

Roxanne learned that the life of a personal assistant to a successful musician was an interesting and challenging one. It was a door to a new creative world that she hadn't known before. And it was exciting. Once she gave up her ideas of the kind of job she thought she should find, she found a job that was perfect for her.

HEART & SOUL TIP

It's important to take charge of life and not let life take charge of you.

HEART & SOUL TIP

Often, an illness or a setback can be a blessing in disguise.

We are always exactly where we're supposed to be in life, and life will always give us exactly what we need at the moment we need it—if we surrender and open ourselves to it.

Making Creative Changes

Everyone is creative. Creative people are not always artists, writers, poets, actors, and musicians. They're also accountants, nurses, doctors, psychiatrists, plumbers, architects, farmers, chefs, ditch diggers, truck drivers, and salespeople. We are all creative beings and we utilize this creativity in every part of our lives—including our careers.

Creative change can be a vital energy source in any person's life. It can be that extra something he or she needs to feel alive and motivated. People find themselves in dead-end, stifling jobs for all sorts of reasons—money, responsibility, and the belief that "I have to have a normal type of job" can imprison you in a job that's not good for you.

Unfortunately, many people also believe that their artistic inclinations and talents are luxuries—something to be used after work or on the weekends. We don't feel that we have the right to do what we love as our regular job!

In her book *Do What You Love, the Money Will Follow,* Marsha Sinetar explains, "We are not born to struggle through life. We are meant to work in ways that suit us, drawing on our natural talents and abilities as a way to express ourselves and contribute to others. . . . This work is a key to our true happiness and self-expression." We all need creative outlets. Without them, we dry up.

In *The Artist's Way,* Julia Cameron writes "Creativity is an experience—a spiritual experience. Creativity is God's gift to us. Using our creativity is our gift back to God." When you open yourself to spirituality, when you truly listen to your inner self and abandon all the preconceived notions about what you should or shouldn't do, creativity will flourish.

Many of us are creatively blocked. Do you ever hear yourself say any of the following statements?

- "It's too late to pursue a career as a songwriter. I'm too old."
- "I have a family to support. How can I devote all my time to my creative interests?"
- "If I had more money saved up, I could spend all my time doing what I really love, but I just don't have enough money in savings."
- "My family and friends will think I'm crazy."

More than likely, if you're telling yourself these types of things, then you are creatively blocked. Fear is stopping you from taking a chance on being happy. Were you aware of that?

Following is an example of a client who was afraid of change—and yet, she knew if she didn't change, she would die. It was that simple.

Lisa Anton

When Lisa approached our office, she looked tired and sleepy. Yawning, she explained that she was a manager for a worldwide printing company and had spent 15 years working the night shift for this organization. "I'm an artist," she said, "and I'm yearning to be able to do my art full-time and leave this job." She was tired of making budgets, managing people, pressure, and last-minute deadlines. "I never have time to do my artwork and I'm unhappy. In fact, I don't have much time alone at all. I'm on call even on my days off, just in case something is going wrong, and I have to go and resolve the issues."

Lisa had been out of touch with her creative side for 15 years. We worked with her for six months, coaching her and counseling her in every part of her life. We rewrote her resume and marketing materials to target creative, artistic jobs. Then, and this was most crucial, to provide her with a true Heart & Soul career tune-up, we instructed her to schedule alone time to rediscover her creative self.

Lisa felt very off balance because she was out of tune with her inner self, which was driving her to the point of frustration and despair. She was on the edge and she needed help.

We can reclaim our creative energy during "alone" time. Lisa had become almost autonomic in her actions—"like a zombie," she explained. Every day was the same as the day before. She excelled in her job and made a great salary, and as a result, her family and friends thought she was doing well. But she knew that wasn't true.

Lisa was a people pleaser. At first, she felt she was being selfish by wanting this alone time. She was afraid that her friends and family would think she was odd or being indifferent, when actually she was being true to herself. We convinced her that a creative soul needs time for nurturing and that we are all creative souls.

After spending some time alone, Lisa began painting again and found new joy—the kind of joy that she remembered from long ago. Finally, after spending a couple of weeks faithfully attending to her alone time and enjoying painting, Lisa realized that she had to be true to her heart—to herself. She knew she had to quit her job. She was no longer afraid. Getting in tune with her inner self had released old fears and superstitions about being employed. She knew that painting was the thing she had been born to do. It was her mission—her higher purpose. She knew that she could use her art to heal others.

So Lisa devoted herself to painting. Quitting her full-time job, she said that she had faith that the money would come somehow, and after a couple of months, it did. One afternoon she met a woman in a grocery store. Casually, the two began to talk, and the woman confided that she had just opened an art gallery. Lisa said, "What a coincidence! I just happen to be a painter!" The woman asked Lisa to bring in some of her paintings so she could get a look at her work. Lisa was thrilled. She took half a dozen oil paintings to the owner, who immediately placed them in her gallery. Within one week, all the paintings were sold!

This might seem miraculous, but it isn't. If you surrender yourself to spirit, the doors will open for you. Life has a way of giving you what you need and want—as long as you don't interfere and block it. Lisa had quit her job because she believed life would take care of her, and it did. Spending time alone had opened her heart to her creative energies. It had given her the strength to believe in herself and overcome her fears of change.

HEART & SOUL TIP

Nothing is keeping you from a fulfilling life and career but yourself.

Not only did Lisa have success with her creative efforts, but she also met the love of her life—another painter. The couple started a company that used healing art in hospitals and schools.

Lisa had taken the leap of faith and quit her stifling job in order to pursue her dreams. And you can do it, too. Nothing is keeping you from a fulfilling life and career but yourself.

Making Unplanned Changes (When Your Job Is Eliminated)

Many people experience crisis after crisis during their careers. Losing your job can be one of the most troubling events you'll ever encounter. No doubt, when your job is eliminated, you're going to feel a little disappointed, maybe even angry. This is one of the most common career changes people face. It happens; it's part of life. And when it happens, we are often left feeling unworthy of anything good. Why else would they eliminate my job or fire me? I must not be important or they would have kept me.

CAREER SUCCESS STORY

Dustin Tyler

"Panic was my first response when I learned that my position had been eliminated after another company bought us out," Dustin Tyler said. He had been a publicist for a company in Chicago for five years. "I'm a single parent with two kids and my job was our sole source of income. I have been scared to death since I learned that my job was eliminated. I immediately wondered why. Wasn't I an important part of the team? All of these questions of self-doubt began to plague me. Not only was my income gone, but so was my self-worth, my self-esteem."

We often see people who have been downsized or eliminated from a position. We explained to Dustin that it was now time to grow and to turn his problems into opportunities. Dustin was confused. "How can I grow and turn this problem into an opportunity when all I can do is worry?"

We told him to use his worry energy in a positive way, to redirect the worry as a positive force and focus first on his inner strength and inner passions.

"Reach deep down within yourself and explore your dreams. Make new goals. You can view this as an opportunity to do something better and to make more money."

Dustin knew that he needed a Heart & Soul career tune-up. He had been out of the job market for five years and didn't know what to expect in today's market.

We rewrote Dustin's resume and prepared his job-searching tools. We then researched employers and key decision makers for him—being a single parent with two children, Dustin simply didn't have hours to spend in the library researching companies. We also videotaped an interview with him and counseled him on dressing for success as well as on his verbal responses.

HEART & SOUL TIP

Redirect your worry energy into a positive force and focus on your inner strength and your inner passions.

We asked Dustin all of the typical questions employers ask. As we explained to Dustin, whenever you interview, you're going to be asked these questions and more, so be prepared. Mock up your own interview and role-play with a friend. Keep your answers short and to the point, and never elaborate unless the interviewer asks you to. Let the interviewer lead and do most of the talking.

Part of any Heart & Soul career tune-up is an honest assessment of yourself. This should happen before you go to your first interview. Many people are incapable of pursuing any long-term goal because they're emotionally immature or just not able to examine their lives deeply enough to uncover who they really are. It's easy for them to grow hopeless and cling to the security of the familiar, no matter what the cost. Big dreams that ask them to move forward are foreboding. But Dustin was being forced to move on. He had no choice.

During one of our counseling sessions, we noticed that Dustin was being negative about himself. We explained to him that it was necessary to accentuate the positive and to modify his negative attitudes. "You have to change your negative image of yourself," we told Dustin. "You have to focus on the positive, and one way to do this is by using affirmations."

HEART & SOUL TIP

Part of any Heart & Soul career tune-up is an honest assessment of yourself.

We worked extensively with Dustin to help him change his attitude using affirmations and to encourage him to use this career change as a positive step in his career. As we continued working with Dustin, we also noticed that he was often exhausted. So we encouraged him to exercise. We told him that his body needed tuning up, just like his career. Simple exercises can help you master any change, whether it's a career change or a personal change.

Various studies have shown that people who exercise have more physical energy and feel better emotionally. Dustin told us that he loved to play basketball; we urged him to join a basketball team at the local YMCA. He began to play three nights a week and told us, "I can't believe how energized I feel after a couple of hours playing basketball. Plus, I've toned up and feel more attractive and confident when I go on interviews."

Eventually, a combination of affirmations, positive change, and exercise improved Dustin's attitude and enabled him to more successfully master his career change. It wasn't long before Dustin found a great job as a publicity director for a large sports arena. This excited him because it was the kind of job he had been dreaming about for years. After putting all of our career strategies into action, Dustin was successful. Like many of our clients, he had learned how to master change, and this had been vital to his Heart & Soul career tune-up.

Taking Inventory

Taking an emotional and professional inventory builds your confidence and inner strength. It helps you focus on your job search and enables you to more successfully master the change.

We recognize that nearly everyone experiences some negative feelings when he or she loses a job, for whatever reason. It's only natural. (We also know that some people are delighted! If you are one of them, congratulations! You are probably very good at celebrating life every day and living in the moment!) Shock, stress, anger, sadness, numbness, anxiety, sleepless nights, headaches, depression, and stomach pain are some of the typical symptoms that can occur as a result of the stress of losing a job. But all of these symptoms will diminish as you take positive strides in your job hunt. As you transform stress energy into active energy, and as you take a proactive approach toward your career, you will build your confidence and self-esteem. You will grow and develop. And you will turn those problems into opportunities.

After you lose a job, it's important to be as positive and as productive as possible. Build your self-esteem and fortify your inner strength by reading and rereading positive evaluations and comments people have written about you. Review customer appreciation letters, glowing letters of recommendation, performance appraisals, and awards. Read these each morning, in the middle of the day, and in the evening so you can stay upbeat about your search for a new job. Believe it or not, this really does help. It reinforces the inner belief that you are the wonderful person you truly are.

"Know yourself before you sell yourself," advises Richard Nelson Bolles, author of the well-known career guide *What Color Is Your Parachute?* "You can't sell your strongest points to others until you're completely familiar with them yourself." Before beginning a job search, Bolles recommends that you ask yourself a few questions. We've highlighted these questions in Worksheet 6.1 for you to answer as honestly as possible—plus we've added some of our own questions. Spend some time on each question and completely fill the space provided with your answers. This exercise will help you focus on yourself.

HEART & SOUL TIP

Build your self-esteem and fortify your inner strength by reading and rereading positive evaluations and comments people have written about you

What are my interests (for example, writing, selling)?

What describes my work style (for example, methodical, creative)?

■ **WORKSHEET 6.1**
Taking Inventory

What skills do I bring to a job (for example, planning, programming)?

What kind of work makes me happiest?

■ **WORKSHEET 6.1 CONTINUED**
Taking Inventory

What kinds of people do I like to work with?

What kind of hours do I like? Flexible or routine, set hours?

What kind of job do I need next that will contribute to both my long-term and short-term goals?

What kind of job will be in tune, or in line, with my Heart & Soul goals—my higher purpose?

■ **WORKSHEET 6.1 CONTINUED**
Taking Inventory

Create your own positive evaluations of good things that have happened in your life. One client told us that whenever she felt depressed, she got out a notebook and wrote down all the wonderful things people had ever said about her or done for her. This simple act always helped her overcome depression and focus on the positive. It never failed to make her smile.

You can also use "selective perception" to concentrate on your positives and ignore the negatives. Start by writing short sentences about the contributions you've made in your career, regardless of why you left your job or were let go. For example:

- "I have increased profits."
- "I have cut costs dramatically."
- "I have developed and implemented several outstanding programs that have increased office efficiency."
- "I can communicate with all levels of management and personnel, and different cultures."
- "I am very dependable. My bosses and associates know they can trust me and depend on me."
- "I can manage multiple projects simultaneously."

When you're going through a change as dramatic as losing a job, it's important to use affirmations to achieve a focused state of mind and to shut out negative distractions. You can use affirmations to change self-defeating attitudes into strong, supportive, and encouraging inner dialogue. Thoughts are real energy. You are what you think you are.

It's vital to have a good attitude in every part of life. As Robert H. Schuller, notable minister and author, said, "It's not what happens to me that matters most; it's how I react to what happens to me."

> **HEART & SOUL TIP**
>
> *Use "selective perception" to concentrate on your positives and ignore the negatives.*

You have the power to choose how you react to life's situations and to change. You have the power to choose your attitude. Despite being unemployed, choose to be optimistic. Look at this career change as an opportunity to do something new. Realize that the power is within you; tap into that power and become the person you want to be. Use this time to do a real overall Heart & Soul career tune-up.

In Worksheet 6.2, list your own positive thoughts, or affirmations, about yourself.

Dream Messages

Since people often feel lost when they lose a job or are trying to find a better career, they need all the tools they can get to help them understand their time of crisis and change. Another tool for mastering change is your "dream messages." Your nightly dreams are a way to connect with your inner divine guidance, with the creative source, your higher power. In her book *Do What You*

POSITIVE THOUGHTS/AFFIRMATIONS

1.

2.

3.

4.

5.

6.

7.

8.

9.

10.

11.

12.

13.

14.

15.

■ **WORKSHEET 6.2**
Positive Thoughts About Me

Love, the Money Will Follow, Marsha Sinetar explains that "dreams can point us in the right direction when we are lost and can let us see the emerging self."

Gayle Delaney, a noted dream therapist and author of *Living Your Dreams*, suggests that, prior to sleep, people ask themselves for the kind of dream they wish to have. By asking for the dream, you are giving permission to your higher, divine power—your inner guidance—to give you information you need. It may take several nights of making this request before you receive and *remember* the answer.

HEART & SOUL TIP

If you don't understand your dream messages at first, keep writing them down and pay attention to the little details. In time, you will begin to understand their true meaning and how they are guiding you in your life.

We suggest you keep a pad and pen on your bedside table. When you wake up in the middle of the night, write down what you just dreamed. Chances are, you won't remember the dream when you wake up the next morning. If you've written it down, it will be there for you to read.

If you don't understand your dreams at first, keep writing them down and pay attention to the little details. In time, you will begin to understand them and know how they are guiding you in your life.

CAREER SUCCESS STORY

Gregory Clapton

Gregory Clapton had been a client of ours for several years. When he was downsized from his position as a sales manager for a pharmaceutical company, he felt desolate. "I really have no idea where to turn or what to do," he told us.

We counseled Gregory for a couple of months, trying to build positive career plans for him. Finally he confided to us one day, "I keep having this recurring dream. I'm in a truck and driving on this road. I'm going really fast when all of a sudden I come to a stop sign and have to put on my brakes. I get out of the truck and look around. On the road are two signs. One points east and one points west. The one pointing west is new and shiny, but the one pointing east is torn up and battered looking. I'm not sure what this dream means or if it has any significance."

We encouraged Gregory to listen to his dreams. These messages won't steer us wrong and can be very helpful in giving us clues as to our next ventures. "What do you think the dream is trying to tell you?" we asked him.

"I believe it's telling me to go west," he said. "I've wanted to move to Colorado all my life, but I never felt like I could leave my family and friends—or my secure job. I have family in the East, in New York, and they have begged me to come there and look for work, but I believe I would suffocate in New York. It's just too big."

"It's obvious that your dream is telling you that Colorado—out West—is the better choice," we explained. "The sign telling you to go west is all shiny and nice. The sign pointing to the east (New York) is dirty and torn up, pointing to a life of difficulty."

"I believe you're right," he said. "I just didn't know if I could trust my dreams to be telling me the truth."

"That's the one thing you can trust," we said. "Our dreams are a connection to inner guidance. Trust them."

As a result of his dreams, Gregory sold his home and moved to Colorado. His family thought he was crazy because he knew no one in Colorado and had no job prospects. They pleaded with him to move to New York where he would be given a job and would be among family members. But Gregory listened to his dreams.

After seven monhs, Gregory called to let us know that he had never been happier in his life. He had found a new career in computer information sytems and had met a wonderful woman. If he had not listened to his dream messages he might well be in New York and living a very unfulfilled, unhappy life.

Not all of one's dreams will be so clear and specific. Often they're shrouded in vague images and activities. They're often ethereal, fuzzy memories of our nightly jaunts into other worlds. However, if you write down your dreams regularly and study them, then you will begin to see a pattern and will understand their messages.

HEART & SOUL TIP

You are your best interpreter when it comes to analyzing your dreams.

Remember, you and only you are your best interpreter when it comes to analyzing your dreams. All the dream books in the world won't be as good at interpreting the message as you will be. We are all individual, unique souls, and our dreams are unique. No common list of dream symbols can accurately describe your dreams.

Reinventing Yourself

*Nothing bad is going to happen to us. If we get
fired, it's not failure; it's a midlife vocational
reassessment.*

P. J. O'ROURKE

THE ONE THING THAT remains constant, no matter what your age, is the need to change. If you try to market yourself based on skills you developed early but haven't continually updated, you may find yourself in a career rut. Entire industries change and sometimes even die in a matter of years. Skills and talents that were once state-of-the-art could soon be out of demand. You must constantly strive to reinvent yourself and update your career skills throughout your life. This is the seventh secret to your Heart & Soul career tune-up!

Throughout this chapter we will explore how and why you need to constantly reinvent yourself throughout your career years. This could mean doing research, getting ongoing training, or maybe pursuing a graduate degree. Sometimes your career needs evolve naturally, which might require you to realign your new goals with your employer's goals. It might mean working for an entirely new department or company. It might mean staying in the same industry, or you might dive into a new industry altogether. But always, you'll need to make changes to keep up with the changing market and your changing needs.

**CAREER
ROAD
BLOCK
STORY**

Barbara Sanders

Barbara Sanders went back to school in 1979 when the youngest of her three children was 16 years old. She chose to study database management and computer programming because she had heard it was going to be the next big thing. Good grades had been few and far between when she went to college the first time—years before—but this time around she was inspired to excel in class. Overall, she told us that going back to school was a rewarding and confidence-building experience for her. In 1981, she graduated with a 3.98 GPA from the two-year technical school. Barbara had successfully reinvented herself and built an entirely new career right in the middle of her life. But the story is not over yet.

Immediately after she graduated, a large company with a growing computer center hired her. She worked diligently for eight years as her soon-to-be-troubled employer dumped more and more work and responsibility on her desk. After some counseling and wise advice, she determined that her employer was asking way too much of her and paying way too little. She made a decision to leave the company. Her husband was a breadwinner as well, so she could afford a little time off without worrying about meeting financial obligations.

Barbara's time off extended longer than she had originally anticipated, and it wasn't until five years later that she decided to throw her hat back in the ring and begin a new job search. But Barbara had failed to realize that in five years, the computer programming industry had changed dramatically. What she had learned in school was nothing compared to what was expected of programmers in the current market.

After being absent so many years from the business, Barbara was lost. Her skills were completely outdated because she had failed to keep pace with the changes in the industry. No company would hire her for what she thought she was worth. Without a current programming skill set, her market value was minimal and the types of jobs she could get amounted to data entry or some basic programming.

HEART & SOUL TIP

You must strive to reinvent yourself year after year after year!

Barbara had done a great job of reinventing herself the first time, but she had failed to keep pace with the changes in the market after she left her last employer. She needed not only to reinvent herself once, but to be constantly reinventing herself year after year!

Judy Allen

Judy Allen met her husband, Cory, a successful architect and a well-respected modern home designer, after college when they had both moved to the same city. They were introduced by one of Judy's college roommates, who thought they would make a cute couple. They did. A week after their first date, they seriously committed to each other. One year later they were engaged. Since Judy was just beginning her residency as a pediatrician, they decided not to get married until she started her own private practice.

Four years later, Cory and Judy had only been back from their honeymoon one month when Judy told Cory she was pregnant. Cory was thrilled. They decided to celebrate with gourmet pizza and videos in front of the fire. Cory called in the order for the pizza and left to pick it up. Tragically, Cory never came home. When Judy playfully answered the insistent doorbell a short time later, thinking it was Cory being silly, she opened the door to a very somber uniformed police officer. She felt her legs give out and she immediately burst into tears. The officer could barely tell her the awful news that Cory had been killed by a drunk driver.

Two years later, a very poised Judy walked into our office because she needed help with her career. After several meetings we became close enough for her to tell us her very personal and tragic story. She said after the accident she had never gone back to work. From a practical standpoint, however, she and her now 18-month-old son, Jason, needed income. Cory's life insurance policy had run out and she was beginning to get worried.

Judy was strong and determined, and she was ready to move on. She said she didn't mind pediatrics, which is what she'd always wanted to do, but she had to have meaning and substance in her work. Although she had gone to medical school just wanting to make good money, things were different now, very different. Money was still necessary, but only as a means to an end. She knew she had something to offer both as a physician and as a human being. She just needed to make her reentry into the working world a meaningful one.

Judy's need to reinvent herself and her career was at a critical point. Her personal renaissance, if you will, had less to do with gaining new training or skills than with her spiritual enlightenment. Judy needed strength and courage to move forward and a tangible career goal that would put meaning back into her professional life.

Throughout this chapter we will explore how and why you need to constantly reinvent yourself throughout your career. This might mean pursuing ongoing training, or maybe a graduate degree. Your career might need to evolve naturally, which might require you to realign your new goals with your employer's. It might mean working for an entirely new department or company. You might stay in the same industry, or you might dive into a new industry altogether.

The passion and energy that drive you are so important that when the little fire inside you starts to die down, you need to reignite it. Judy had worked hard to become a pediatrician, and financially she couldn't afford to go into another field, but she wasn't inspired by her work as much as she had thought she would be. She really wanted to teach and help others. Practically, she also needed to make $70,000 a year.

Together, we came up with a successful solution. It wasn't the "silver bullet" answer, but her new plan evolved. Judy was very unsure of herself and her new commitments at first, but logically it all made sense. Only after she began to work did she begin to feel the flame inside of her light up again.

Judy did not go into private practice as she had originally intended. Instead, she chose to teach at the local university hospital. She loved working with the young doctors and helping them pursue their dreams. The university also allowed her to take a one-month sabbatical every year so she could work for a charitable organization, pro bono, in a developing country. Helping people in isolated communities who have never had professional medical attention was deeply rewarding to her. She grew to love her work and became extremely passionate about her efforts abroad.

Avenues for Change

Some of our clients worry that they don't have enough money to go back to school and that they will never be able to improve their financial position in life. They feel stuck and their real-life goals seem too far out of reach. Some have identified the need to reinvent themselves, but they still try to find reasons why they are not good candidates for change.

If you find yourself worrying about your abilities to reinvent yourself, keep this in mind: Everything you need to know is available in inexpensive books or journals. We can't tell you where to go or how to get the information you need, but if you have the desire to seek out and absorb the knowledge you need to further your career, you'll find it. Whether your knowledge comes in the form of formal education, trade school, weekend workshops, or self-study, you need to be a sponge ready to soak up every tidbit!

HEART & SOUL TIP

Everything you need to know is available in inexpensive books or journals. If you have the desire to seek out and absorb the knowledge you need to further your career, you'll find it.

Although before you begin, you need to ask yourself straightforward questions about your desire to gain additional education, you also need to allow time and energy for your heart and soul. The financial part of your education is the easiest part of the equation. Capturing the essence of your heart and soul as you reinvent yourself, however, demands a deep understanding of your desires and motivations. You must approach this part of your change with a much more profound energy and enthusiasm.

Educational resources are bountiful, and you will always be able to update your skills if you are motivated. Going to school or to the library is the easy part. The difficult part is making the commitment to pursue a new or higher level in your career.

Sometimes the need to change is not so obvious. For example, your job and your industry may be going great guns now, but in today's fast- and ever-changing world, both could be uprooted in only a few years. Or funding could dry up or market demand for your expertise could dwindle. The bottom line is that you really don't know what is going to happen in the future, so you need to be prepared to move onward and upward. Whether you love your job or you're ready to quit tomorrow, you need to have an exit strategy and a personal growth plan for your heart and soul and for your career.

Employer Versus Industry Issues

If you're not happy in your present position, try to identify why. You probably don't want or need to make dramatic life and career changes when the problem is really just a bad boss or employer. Maybe you're not getting paid enough, maybe you're not challenged, or maybe you're bored and restless. Before you begin your personal renaissance, you need to explore your career as it is now. Specifically, you need to understand what you like and dislike about your current employer. It's important not to confuse career dissatisfaction with employer dissatisfaction. Your career tune-up could be as simple as working for a competitor that aligns more closely with your values and skill set.

Answer the questions below about your current employer. Answering "no" to more than a few of these questions is a red flag that the match between you and your employer is not good. In completing this exercise, don't assess blame. You are not a bad employee and your employer is not necessarily a bad employer. You just may not fit well with each other. The solution could be as simple as a reassignment to a different department.

How Do You Rate Your Employer?

Take a minute to answer the following questions about your current employer.

- Is your compensation satisfactory to you?
- Are your personal and career goals aligned with your employer's?
- Do you have substantial career growth opportunities?
- Do you respect and admire your company leaders?
- Do you respect your peers?
- Do you respect your subordinates?
- Do you fit into your company's culture?
- Are you managed, supervised, or monitored well?
- Are you in control of areas for which you have decision-making responsibility?
- Do you enjoy going to work?
- Are you excited about your work?

Now, based on your answers and the important job satisfaction issues behind these questions, answer the four question sets in Worksheet 7.1 on the next four pages. The idea is to clearly understand the difference between employer-related issues and industry-related issues. For example, if you are dissatisfied with your employer alone, your career tune-up is a simple step away—perhaps a marginal or incremental boost in training to get hired by a competitor. However, if the issues you have with your employer pervade your entire industry, maybe it's time to consider a more dramatic move. You'll want to aggressively retrain yourself in a new skill set.

Professional Heart & Soul Questions

We talk about heart and soul on an emotional and personal level, but for your career we need to talk about it on a professional level as well. From this perspective, what do you want from your employer? How do you want customers to respond to you and your employer? How do you want to feel when you are at work? What will be the basis for your professional relationships at work?

HEART & SOUL TIP

You must know what is in your heart and soul before you search for a company with the same mind-set.

You need to confidently answer questions like these before you can fairly assess any potential employer. You can't fairly judge any company before you know yourself. That is, you must know what is in your heart and soul before you go searching for a company with the same mind-set.

The *reactive* approach is to send out resumes, get a job, and then a few months or years down the road decide you're just not a good match for the company. That's a big waste of time! The *proactive* approach is to thoroughly understand yourself and what you want to achieve, and *then* research companies with a mission and culture that align with your own.

By tapping into your heart and soul, you can gain a huge advantage over the employers and your peers who are vying for similar positions. Your

HEART & SOUL TIP

By tapping into your heart and soul, you can gain a huge advantage over the employers and your peers who are vying for similar positions.

advantage over the employer comes with the *asymmetry* of information. This means that you know more about the company and your motivation to work there than the company knows about you. Assuming you have found the right company to work for, you can use this asymmetry to your advantage. Aggressively sell yourself to the employer by communicating your fundamental understanding of the company's culture and mission. Sell the company on who you are as an individual and how your vision aligns closely with the employer's. You will practically have the job offer wrapped up in a matter of days!

For you to successfully reinvent yourself, you must do the following:

- Define the strengths and weaknesses of your current employer.
- Define the strengths and weaknesses of your current industry.
- Define your professional ambitions, personal goals, and vision.
- Determine your most logical career path.

HEART & SOUL QUESTIONS

What do you like and dislike about your current employer?
(Note: Do not list items that are indicative of all companies in your industry. Isolate the problems specific to your current employer.)

Like

Dislike

HEART & SOUL QUESTIONS

What do you like and dislike about your industry?
(Note: Do not list items that are indicative of your employer. Isolate the problems specific to your industry.)

Like

Dislike

HEART & SOUL QUESTIONS

What do you want out of your next career move?
(Note: List everything that you want to gain by making a career move, either internally in your company or externally to another employer. Prioritize the items on your list.)

Internal Career Move

External Career Move

HEART & SOUL QUESTIONS

What industries and companies offer what you desire?
(Note: Based on your answers to the previous questions, think about what you want to change in your career and list the industries and companies that could potentially offer these things. Answering this question may require more in-depth research—see Chapter 3 for help on researching employers and industries.)

■ **WORKSHEET 7.1 CONTINUED**
Employer Versus Industry Issues

- Take necessary informal training and/or pursue more formal degree-based education.
- Align your vision and goals with those of a heart-and-soul-based employer.

Formal Education

Academia: preparation for reality or an escape from reality? The answer depends on who you ask, where you go to school, and what major you're considering. For our purposes, formal education will be any education received at any accredited school offering associate, bachelor's, master's, and/or doctoral degree programs. These programs will provide the basis and foundation for most new career directions you might consider.

From a financial perspective, you want to be able to justify the expense by commanding a higher salary, right? You want a good rate of return on the investment of your money and time in education. The benefit of formal education is that it signals to employers and colleagues that you care deeply about your career and that you were willing to commit significant time, money, and effort to earning a degree. Even if your area of study doesn't exactly match the employer's needs, your degree signals to the employer that you are a committed and intelligent person.

Formal education offers challenging curriculum and interaction with peers in the same course of study. It forces you to shift your thinking, strengthen your weaknesses, and learn the most up-to-date systems, thinking, and technology available in your field. You also get to study under professors who may later act as advisors or mentors in your career.

HEART & SOUL TIP

You can determine whether going back to school is a good financial investment by using a formula; however, determining the Heart & Soul investment is not so easy.

Money and time not being issues, we strongly encourage continued formal education. Unfortunately, though, money and time are issues for most of us, especially as we progress in age. Our priorities shift, and time and money become much more valuable in satisfying the basic physical and emotional needs of ourselves and our families. You need to balance the costs and benefits of additional education with personal and family commitments.

The formula to determine the financial value of a formal education is described in Worksheet 7.2 on page 124. The higher salary you may command after earning a degree must pay for your initial investment (tuition and books), the money you didn't make while you were in school, and the interest you would have earned on your money had you not invested in school.

The formula in Worksheet 7.2 does not take into account the time value of money, which is an integral part of any investment plan. It also doesn't consider the return on an alternative investment if you were to invest in another asset. Use this formula to stimulate your interest and thought. And consider the many personal and spiritual reasons that go into your continued education decision; don't stifle your spirit by trying to quantify these intangibles. You can get more specific and detailed once you have a basic idea of what you want to

LINE 1 How much (per year) will you spend on school (tuition, books, room, board, etc.)?	
LINE 2 How much would you make (per year) in total after-tax income if you did not attend school?	
LINE 3 Total annual cost of your education.	
LINE 4 Years in your chosen degree program.	
LINE 3 x LINE 4 = Total cost of your education.	

■ **WORKSHEET 7.2**
Financial Analysis Summary of Your Education

accomplish. Seek out additional professional help for more thorough and detailed financial analysis.

To get an idea of the financial rewards you could reap by going back to school, thoroughly analyze the degrees and colleges you might consider using the questions in Table 7.1. Most schools track employment and salary data regarding their alumni, and this information can help you determine your potential value if you were to graduate from the same or a similar program.

HEART & SOUL TIP

We know this fact to be universally true: Upgrading Your Skills = Improved Market Value!

Depending on what industry you're in, a lack of continued education could mean a constant decline or stabilization of your market value. But you want a constant increase in your market value. You want to command a higher salary each year. Compare your net estimated income after your education and opportunity costs are deducted with your net income if you do not receive any additional education. Critically analyze the added value of another degree with the time and money you're going to have to invest.

We know this fact to be universally true: Upgrading Your Skills = Improved Market Value! You need to ask yourself how much you're willing to invest in upgrading your skills. Sometimes upgrading your skills will not entail a new degree. Sometimes you just need some additional informal education.

Informal Education

Workshops, seminars, and self-study educational options are relatively inexpensive or free. You can also work them into your existing lifestyle; for example, you can continue in your current career and study on the side. Some

HEART & SOUL TIP

Identify your career path and training needs before you start attending workshops or studying.

employers will pay for this training, but don't ask them to spend money on skill building that is unrelated to your current job. If you have career interests different from what you are doing now, you need to be prepared to pay for your own education.

Identify your career path and training needs before you start attending workshops or studying. It's important that you directly

- What do graduates with a particular degree make?

- What do graduates with this particular degree, from this particular college, make?

- What other local colleges could I consider?

- Are there executive, part-time, or correspondence colleges to consider?

- What is the range of starting salaries with a particular degree and from a particular college?

- What degrees match my personal mission and career goals?

- What is the cost of the degree?

- How much would I make if I didn't go back to school?

■ **TABLE 7.1**
Questions to Ask When Considering a College and Degree

benefit from your continued education. The same is true for self-study. You need to have a focus before you begin! You will benefit from self-study only if you are entirely dedicated and committed to a certain concentration of study. You want be able to put this on your resume, so focus your study on specific and practical areas. Table 7.2 on page 126 lists some questions that can help you assess your informal education needs.

The Right Career Path

If you leave control of your life and career to chance, they will follow the path of least resistance—just like water. For many of us, as our career unfolds, we feel a natural pull to a certain direction (like water and gravity). Our employer, family, boss, and even peers may "see" us in our future job and subconsciously draw us down a certain, seemingly natural path. We feel at ease when we continue down this same path of least resistance.

The difficulty comes when the easiest career path turns out to not be the best one for us. In finding the right path, you need a clear definition of who you are and what you want to accomplish. You need to constantly strive to reinvent yourself so you can reach the next step in your career.

Your boss may love your work, but she may not see you in a senior management position. She may very subtly encourage you to pursue a less ambitious career direction. Or you may be a successful engineer and everyone assumes you'll move into an advanced engineering position. The problem is, though, that you're tired of working in a cubicle and you want to go into sales! If you don't have a vision of what you want to do, your career will follow the easy path, which may lead to a dead end.

- What do you need to know to improve your market value?

- Where can you find the most accurate, up-to-date information?

- How much will this information cost?

- Does a particular seminar or workshop help you move along your career path?

- How much time are you willing to commit per week, per month, to you continued study?

- Do you need a degree, or do you just need the knowledge?

■ **TABLE 7.2**
Questions to Ask About Your Informal Education

The Career Map

We've discussed the use of a career map in our other *Heart & Soul* books. A career map is a simple and important tool that you can incorporate into your planning to help you visualize how your career will progress.

Our client Scott Bragden recently developed his very simple career map. He looked at where he was—an electrical engineer—and where he wanted to be—senior manager or CEO of a major high-tech firm. He had three options: (1) he could get promoted with his existing employer, (2) he could work for a similar or competing firm and pursue career advancement with another employer, or (3) he could start and grow his own company.

For each of these options Scott knew he would need to get a graduate degree—probably an MBA. He also knew that he would need to build a strong network of contacts and always compete for the best promotions and jobs. Figure 7.1 shows Scott's career map. Use Worksheet 7.3 on page 128 to design your own career map.

Sell Your "New" Self

Your success is based on your ability to sell yourself—in other words, *marketing!* If you have reinvented yourself and are taking off on a new or updated career path, you must let people know! Promote yourself and your new ideas. Market yourself. Sell your colleagues, peers, family, and friends on your new-found commitment. When you have "buy-in" to your new goals, everyone will begin to support you emotionally, send you referrals, or help you out however they can.

Have you or any of your friends ever considered real estate sales? It's a fine profession, but due to the "low barrier" to entry and high turnover in the business, new agents have a hard time

HEART & SOUL TIP

Sell yourself! Wave your own flag! Let people know about you!

■ **FIGURE 7.1**
Career Map for Scott Bragden

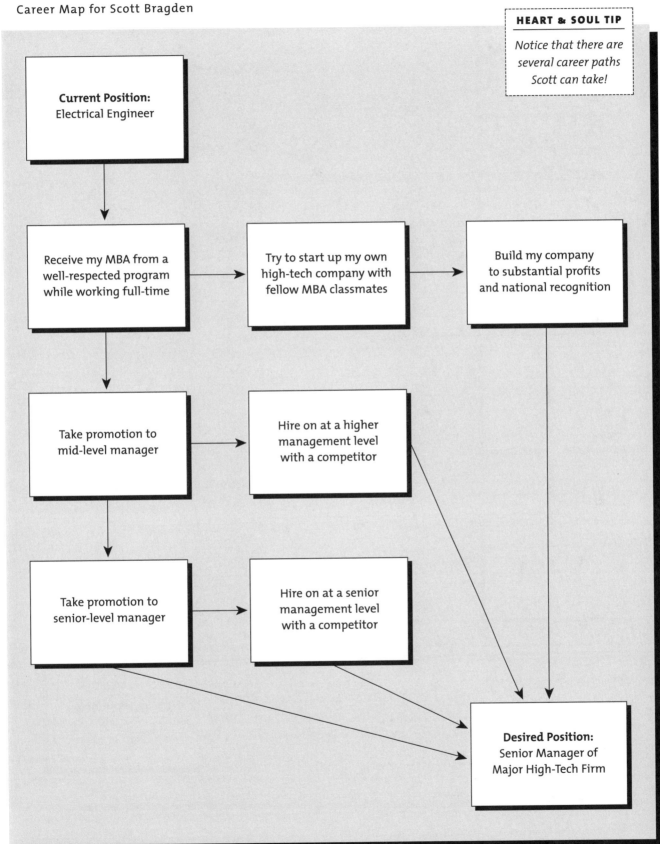

HEART & SOUL TIP

*Notice that there are
several career paths
Scott can take!*

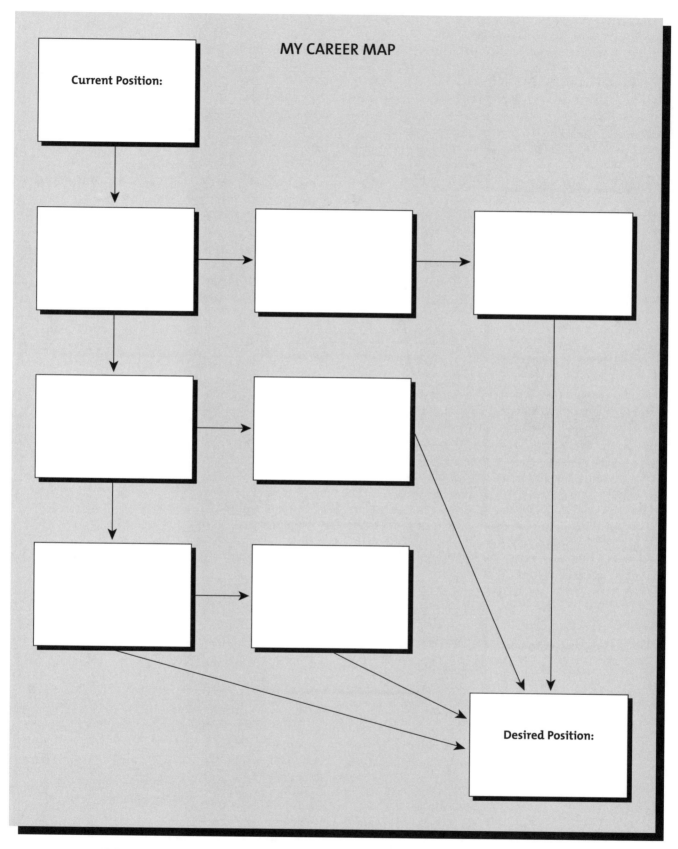

MY CAREER MAP

Current Position:

Desired Position:

■ **WORKSHEET 7.3**
Design Your Own Career Map

- Continually update your skills through formal education or informal training.

- Stay spiritually and emotionally strong.

- Be motivated and prepared for constant change.

- Create a well-defined career map.

- Willingly compete for what you want.

■ **TABLE 7.3**
Key Concepts for Your Personal and Career Renaissance

convincing their potential clients, friends, and family that they are committed to the business. Agents who don't successfully sell themselves in the business have problems getting referrals because people don't have confidence in their skills and/or staying power. However, new agents who start out very aggressively and sell themselves as professionals and experienced agents do much better. People know they are new to the business but admire their "go-get-it" attitude. These agents are not just selling real estate; they're selling themselves.

No matter what your profession, you need to sell yourself. People must believe in you and trust you before they'll do business with you. You want the trust and confidence of everyone you contact. They will benefit from your enthusiasm and excitement and pass that back to you. Enthusiasm is contagious!

Your Renaissance

Reinventing yourself is exciting and rewarding. On a Heart & Soul level, you should be in tune with who you are and what you want, and intellectually you must create a realistic career path to a well-defined career objective. The energy and passion that you need to be a success are alive inside you. It's up to you to ignite the fire that will give you the courage and motivation to change. But it's right there!

HEART & SOUL TIP

Stay current! The competition is always fierce for the best jobs, and you don't want to be left behind!

As illustrated in Table 7.3, throughout your renaissance, you must constantly reinvent yourself and implement Heart & Soul career tune-ups to continue progressing. Plan far enough ahead so that if you need a graduate degree, you can budget your time and money. Make regular trips to the library or a bookstore and read about all the latest issues and trends. Stay current! The competition is always fierce for the best jobs, and you don't want to be left behind!

Life Is Going Great, But . . .

Does this sound familiar? Your career is going great, you're making great money, and, from the outside at least, life seems to be perfect. But there is something missing. Something's out of place and you're not quite sure what's wrong, but life isn't perfect. You feel edgy and out of balance. Perhaps you need to take a deeper look at your inner workings—at the heart and soul of your being—as part of your renaissance.

In any Heart & Soul career tune-up, you must tune up your spirit—your heart and soul—as well as other parts of yourself. You do know, don't you, that you're not a physical body that owns a soul, but rather a soul that owns a physical body? When you come into this life, you take on a physical appearance—a body. This body is your "house" to wear while you are in this existence. You're a spiritual being, not just some physical blueprint that functions like a robotic machine. You're *more* than that, much, much more. And, like all the other parts of yourself and your career, your spirit needs constant tuning up in order to stay in sync and in balance with life.

When you're doing what you love, when the deepest part of you becomes completely immersed in what you're doing, when your activities and actions become heart-and-soul gratifying and purposeful, then you are doing what you were meant to do. You are working for a "higher purpose." You are accomplishing your life's mission. You, as spirit—as heart and soul—are buoyant and in sync, in tune with life. You delight in your work and in others, which enables you to appreciate others' diversity even more.

And just how do you get to this point in your life—the point where you can accept and embrace diversity? If you're not already there, then it's important that you stop and take a good look at yourself. We're sure that if you're reading this book, then you're someone who *wants* to be there. Getting to this point is not an automatic process. It takes several steps and inner soul searching to achieve this higher-caliber way of living, this true Heart & Soul way of life.

We believe that you can handle diversity and reinventing yourself much better if you know yourself as heart and soul. We believe that it's important in your Heart & Soul career tune-up to be totally in alignment with your inner self, as well as in your outer career and everyday world. When you want to reach that inner place within you—that sacred place where God talks to you—there are several Heart & Soul tools you can use. One is simply good old "been around a long time" mainstream meditation.

Dr. Dean Ornish has a meditation program that has successfully reversed heart disease, and this spiritual practice has been hitting the mainstream hard. In today's career world, straitlaced corporations throughout the United States have begun using meditation to increase productivity and decrease the number

HEART & SOUL TIP

People who have practiced transcendental meditation for five years or more have been shown to have higher levels of DHEA, a hormone associated with youth that decreases as people age.

HEART & SOUL TIP

Meditation shouldn't be a chore, but rather something you anticipate with pleasure.

of insurance claims because meditation keeps the employees healthy! Even the American Medical Association has advised patients with borderline high blood pressure to try this method of relaxation before resorting to medication.

Deepak Chopra, M.D., author of 20 books including *The Seven Spiritual Laws of Success,* has discovered that people who practice transcendental meditation for five years or more have higher levels of DHEA, a hormone associated with youth that decreases as people age. Studies have also shown that experienced meditators are far less likely to be hospitalized for any illness, including heart attack.

Meditation is a type of spiritual exercise to help you reach a higher state of consciousness. It is the practice of intense awareness, and it is a very important and effective Heart & Soul tool to use in your career tune-up, as well as in your everyday life. There are several methods that you can easily incorporate into your career world and your daily life. No matter which method you decide to use, before you sit down to practice your meditation exercise, you will ned to prepare yourself and your environment for this sacred, special event. Here are some suggestions to help you get started.

1. Disconnect your phone and hang a Keep Out, Do Not Disturb sign on your door (regardless of whether you're at home or in an office). Lock cats in the bathroom and put your dog outside. (Past experience has shown that some dogs and cats like to curl up with you and meditate alongside you. If this is the case, then by all means, let them join you.) The point is to do whatever it takes to ensure that you won't be disturbed or interrupted.

2. Don't eat before you meditate. It's best if you can meditate on an empty stomach so your body isn't expending energy on digestion.

3. Try meditating first thing in the morning when you wake up or last thing at night before you go to bed. Done in the morning, this meditation/spiritual exercise will help get your day off to a good start. You will be immediately opened up to the creative force of life, and this can bring good things to you throughout the day.

4. Wash your face and hands before beginning to stave off drowsiness.

5. Don't force it. Meditation shouldn't be a chore, but rather something you anticipate with pleasure.

6. If you'd like, enhance your atmosphere by lighting a candle, burning incense, or even playing soft music in the background.

7. If you feel restless, try a form of meditation/spiritual exercise that involves movement, such as hatha yoga, tai chi, or walking meditation.

8. Resist the impulse to give up because you can't seem to sit still. If 20 minutes feels too long, then start with 5 and gradually increase.

9. Experiment until you find the method that works for you. Shift techniques to fit different needs. For example, practice meditation when you're stressed out about work and visualization to cope with a sports injury.

10. Find an experienced mentor to guide you.

OK, now you've completed all your preliminary steps to meditation exercises. No matter which meditation method you choose, you need to incorporate the following steps.

1. Relax and get comfy. Sitting either on the floor or in a chair with both feet resting on the floor, keep your back straight. Don't lie down unless you need help relaxing. Loosen any constrictive clothing so you can breathe freely.

2. Close your eyes. Take a few breaths and relax. Tell yourself that for the next 20 minutes, you are going to devote all your attention to yourself. This is your private time and no one else can interfere with it.

3. Relax your body. Take a mental survey of all your body parts, especially your chest, neck, and facial muscles. Notice where you're the most tense. Each time you breathe in and exhale, imagine the muscles loosening up. Silently tell those muscles to just *let go*. Feel all the tension draining from your muscles.

4. Notice your surroundings. For a few moments, pay attention to the ambient sounds, the touch of the chair against your body, the floor beneath your feet, the clothes against your skin. Do you hear birds singing outside? Perhaps the wind is blowing ever so lightly, gently ruffling through the trees. Do you hear any other noises, such as a clock ticking or a refrigerator humming? Acknowledge these noises and then let them go.

5. Focus. Now, turn your attention inward. Allow your mind to settle on a focal point. Concentrate on your third inner eye, which is the space directly between your eyes. Repeat a mantra either outwardly (vocally) or inwardly (silently). You can repeat one of the various mantras including OM, AUM, or HU, which are ancient names for God. It really doesn't make any difference what mantra you choose.

6. Sit still. Keep your body as motionless as possible. When you feel the urge to move, notice your physical sensations and wait for them to diminish in intensity. If you're in pain and think you'll die unless you shift positions instantly, then do it. Just move slowly. Or, if parts of your body need attention, then address the need. For example, if you notice your nose is itching and this is distracting you from your meditation/spiritual exercise, then scratch it. Then dismiss it and get back to your focus.

7. Refocus. The instant you become aware that you're thinking about something else, repeat your mantra and concentrate on your focal point—your third eye. Mindfulness and walking meditators should acknowledge their straying thoughts by just silently repeating their mantra.

8. Resist drowsiness. If you start getting drowsy, straighten your spine and move away from a back support. Resist the urge to curl up and go to sleep. (Sometimes a meditative/spiritual exercise is good to do before you go to bed at night, because it does relax you and puts you in a wonderful state for sleeping.)

9. Come back. After about 20 minutes, come back. You can peek at a clock to see if your allotted time is over. After you practice doing these spiritual exercises a few times, you will inwardly know when 20 minutes are up. You can slowly introduce your body to movement by wiggling your toes and fingers or gently stretching your arms. Open your eyes. You have just completed a wonderful meditation/spiritual exercise which is effective in tuning up your heart and soul.

Mind and Intellectual Check-up in the Workplace

Perhaps, like many others today, you are unhappy because you haven't addressed your needs as a Heart & Soul being in the workplace. More and more people are seeking personal growth and creative expression in their jobs. They want to work in a place that nurtures them and gives them freedom to evolve into better human beings. That's not always easy to find, but it's very important in our world. In the process, sooner or later, they will have to venture out of their comfortable (albeit boring) jobs and look for something in the workplace that is directly aligned with their life's mission, their vocation.

HEART & SOUL TIP

More and more people want to worrk in a place that nurtures them and gives them freedom to evolve into better human beings..

In her book *Holy Work,* Marsha Sinetar states, "Our daily labor, approached rightly, devotionally, can help us come into our fullness of being as unique individuals within the unit of a larger existence. Ultimately, as we affirm God's summons, we become willing servants of Life's purposes, and not only our daily work but we ourselves reflect that which is of God's infinitude."

In other words, if you are doing the work you are meant to do in life—your calling, your vocation, your higher purpose—then you are truly serving life's grander scheme. There is no better life and there is no better way to fulfill your role on Earth than to be working directly as a co-worker with life itself.

CAREER SUCCESS STORY

Chelsea Brown

Chelsea Brown discovered how important it was to work in an environment that embraced diversity, allowed creative expression, and encouraged holistic and intellectual growth. She had spent several years working as an agent for large film companies in Los Angeles. The money was exceptional, and she lived life in the fast lane—she was hardly ever home except to sleep or to change her clothes. Her film company owned her, body and soul. Although she appeared very successful outwardly, she knew she was dying on the inside.

"I need an environment that is slower," she told us, "a place that focuses more on my needs as well as the company's. If I show my employers how creative I am, I don't think I will be accepted in the company. I want a place that will nurture my creative diversity—a place that allows my creative side to develop."

After extensive counseling and Heart & Soul searching, Chelsea decided to set up her own business as a counselor and agent for struggling actors and actresses—people who weren't successful yet and who needed encouragement and support. Her salary was cut in half when she made this change. But having her own business meant that she could design her days any way she wanted. It gave her the freedom to be as diverse and creative as she wanted, to express her creativity to the max, and to fulfill her higher purpose in life—helping actors and actresses who really needed help.

Today, Chelsea is part of a growing number of workers with radically different attitudes about work, who are transforming traditional concepts of loyalty and career advancement. If companies aren't willing to accept and embrace these diverse individuals, these individuals will simply chart their own courses.

> **HEART & SOUL TIP**
>
> *Viewing work as a place to grow and develop, not just a place to draw a paycheck, is the major difference between the worker of the future and the traditional employee of a few generations ago.*

Viewing work as a place to grow and develop, not just a place to draw a paycheck, is the major difference between the worker of the future and the employee of a generation or two ago. Personal growth, based on personal goals, dreams, and lifetime missions, is becoming more and more important.

Finding meaning in your job isn't a new concept, but it is more prevalent today than ever before. Most people are likely to go through a string of companies during their careers. No longer can we depend on one company for a lifetime of work. As a result, people are looking inward to find the satisfaction and peace that will make them happy.

When you're venturing through your Heart & Soul career tune-up, reevaluate your intentions, your goals, and your dreams. Tune in to your inner self. Embrace life. Embrace those who are different and learn from them. These are all integral, synergistic facets of your mind/intellectual checkup and will benefit you greatly in your Heart & Soul career tune-up.

Au Revoir!

We have taken you on an inner and outer journey in this book to help you recognize and understand different facets of yourself that contribute to your overall success or failure in your career and in life. All of our strategies work together in a synergistic, holistic way to create a true Heart & Soul approach toward yourself, your career, and your life.

Life is an exciting journey, full of wonders and possibilities. It's up to you to recognize this, embrace it, and achieve your maximum potential in this lifetime. Whatever you choose to do on your life's journey and in your career, we wish you well. We wish you success and much happiness in your career and personal life. Above all, we wish you love.

Using the Myers-Briggs Type Indicator Instrument to Guide Your Career Tune-Up

The *Myers-Briggs Type Indicator®* (MBTI®) instrument is an invaluable tool in a Heart & Soul career tune-up. By combining your personality characteristics (as illustrated in the MBTI instrument) with your skills and experience developed over a lifetime, you can transform your tune-up into one with real heart and soul.

The MBTI instrument must be administered and interpreted by a counseling professional, who not only will interpret the results of the instrument but also will discuss with you and analyze other issues in your life that are pertinent to your career and life decisions. Call a career counselor for more information. For immediate purposes, if you haven't used the MBTI instrument, following are a brief history and some basic concepts that may help you right away when preparing a Heart & Soul resume.

History of the Myers-Briggs Type Indicator (MBTI) Instrument

The MBTI personality inventory was developed by Isabel Myers and Katharine Briggs to make Carl Jung's theory of psychological types understandable and useful in people's lives. Jung believed that many of the apparently random differences in people's behavior were actually a result of their preferred modes of perception and judgment. Perception refers to how you gather information, while judgment refers to how you come to conclusions based on what you have perceived. There are two opposite ways of perceiving, through Sensing or Intuition, and likewise two opposite ways of forming judgments, through Thinking or Feeling. Jung referred to these two pairs of opposites as the *functions*. He also described differences in the ways people prefer to focus these functions and identified another pair of opposites, which he called Extraversion and Introversion. Myers and Briggs, when constructing the MBTI instrument, added a fourth dichotomy that they thought was implicit in Jung's theory. This was the Judging and Perceiving dichotomy, which relates to one's preferences for using either one of the judging functions (Thinking or Feeling) or one of the perceiving functions (Sensing or Intuition) as the primary means of dealing with the outer world.

All of us use all eight preferences at different times. Your MBTI results indicate which of each pair of opposites you most prefer. Together, these four preferences make up what is called your *type*. Your type can be identified by the letters that are associated with your preferences on each of the four dichotomies. For example, if your type is reported as ENFP, this means you indicated preferences for Extraversion, Intuition, Feeling, and Perceiving when you answered the MBTI items.

Table A.1 summarizes the four MBTI dichotomies. Since there are two opposites for each dichotomy, there are a total of eight preferences.

The various combinations of the eight preferences make up 16 different personality types. If you don't already know your type, Table A.2, "Characteristics Frequently Associated with Each Type," may help you in analyzing yours.

Please note that while the names of the MBTI preferences are familiar, in everyday use they have meanings that are different from their MBTI meanings. Remember:

- *Extravert* does not mean "talkative."
- *Introvert* does not mean "shy" or "inhibited."
- *Feeling* does not mean "emotional."
- *Judging* does not mean "judgmental."
- *Perceiving* does not mean "perceptive."

Characteristics Associated with Each MBTI Preference

If you have not yet used the *Myers-Briggs Type Indicator* instrument but have reviewed the above section, you may be able to identify some characteristics or preferences that apply to you. In Table A.3 (page 139) we have compiled characteristics commonly associated with each MBTI preference. Read through each section and mark the characteristics that you believe strongly correlate

Direction of Energy	
Extraversion (E) Focus on the people and things in the outer world	*Introversion (I)* Focus on the thoughts, feelings, and impressions of the inner world

Gathering Information	
Sensing (S) Focus on facts and details that can be confirmed by experience	*Intuition (N)* Focus on possibilities and relationships among ideas

Making Decisions	
Thinking (T) Use impersonal, objective, logical analysis to reach conclusions	*Feeling (F)* Use person-centered, subjective analysis to reach conclusions

Dealing with the Outer World	
Judging (J) Plan and organize; make decisions and come to closure	*Perceiving (P)* Be spontaneous and adaptable; collect information and stay open to new options

From Introduction to Type and Careers, *Allen L. Hammer. Copyright 1993 by Consulting Psychologists Press. Reproduced with permission.*

■ **TABLE A.1**
MBTI Preferences

with your personality and work ethic. Even if a particular characteristic is not in "your type," you still may have developed a certain skill or affinity for it and will want to incorporate it into your resume. Incorporate any relevant phrases into sentences that best describe you. Once you have identified a personal characteristic, think of examples and stories you may tell to illustrate it. Remember, when making a positive comment about yourself, you should always support your statement with real-life illustrations of your success. For example, don't just say, "Excellent communicator." Instead, write, "Excellent communication skills exemplified as a national workshop presenter for special industry trade shows."

Table A.3 lists just a small sampling of characteristics associated with each of the preferences, and Table A.4 lists phrases that describe characteristics resulting from combinations of the preferences. Look at the resources at the back of this book for more detailed information on the MBTI instrument or, as we mentioned earlier, call a career counselor.

Studying the MBTI instrument is an excellent aid to understanding who you are, a necessary component of writing a Heart & Soul resume.

	Sensing Types		Intuitive Types	
Introverts	**ISTJ** Serious, quiet, earn success by concentration and thoroughness. Practical, orderly, matter-of-fact, logical, realistic, and dependable. See to it that everything is well organized. Take responsibility. Make up their own minds as to what should be accomplished and work toward it steadily, regardless of protests or distractions.	**ISFJ** Quiet, friendly, responsible, and conscientious. Work devotedly to meet their obligations. Lend stability to any project or group. Thorough, painstaking, accurate. Their interests are usually not technical. Can be patient with necessary details. Loyal, considerate, perceptive, concerned with how other people feel.	**INFJ** Succeed by perseverance, originality, and desire to do whatever is needed or wanted. Put their best efforts into their work. Quietly forceful, conscientious, concerned for others. Respected for their firm principles. Likely to be honored and followed for their clear vision as to how to best serve the common good.	**INTJ** Have original minds and great drive for their own ideas and purposes. Have long-range vision and quickly find meaningful patterns in external events. In fields that appeal to them, they have a fine power to organize a job and carry it through. Skeptical, critical, independent, determined; have high standards of competence and performance.
Introverts	**ISTP** Cool onlookers—quiet, reserved, observing and analyzing life with detached curiosity and unexpected flashes of original humor. Usually interested in cause and effect, how and why mechanical things work, and organizing facts using logical principles. Excel at getting to the core of a practical problem and finding the solution.	**ISFP** Retiring, quietly friendly, sensitive, kind, modest about their abilities. Shun disagreements, do not force their opinions or values on others. Usually do not care to lead but are often loyal followers. Often relaxed about getting things done because they enjoy the present moment and do not want to spoil it by undue haste or exertion.	**INFP** Quiet observers, idealistic, loyal. Important that outer life be congruent with inner values. Curious, quick to see possibilities, often serve as catalysts to implement ideas. Adaptable, flexible, and accepting unless a value is threatened. Want to understand people and ways of fulfilling human potential. Little concern with possessions or surroundings.	**INTP** Quiet and reserved. Especially enjoy theoretical or scientific pursuits. Like solving problems with logic and analysis. Interested mainly in ideas, with little liking for parties or small talk. Tend to have sharply defined interests. Need careers where some strong interest can be used and useful.
Extraverts	**ESTP** Good at on-the-spot problem solving. Like action, enjoy whatever comes along. Tend to like mechanical things and sports, with friends on the side. Adaptable, tolerant, pragmatic; focused on getting results. Dislike long explanations. Are best with real things that can be worked, handled, taken apart, or put together.	**ESFP** Outgoing, accepting, friendly, enjoy everything and make things more fun for others by their enjoyment. Like action and making things happen. Know what's going on and join in eagerly. Find remembering facts easier than mastering theories. Are best in situations that need sound common sense and practical ability with people.	**ENFP** Warmly enthusiastic, high-spirited, ingenious, imaginative. Able to do almost anything that interests them. Quick with a solution or any difficulty and ready to help anyone with a problem. Often rely on their ability to improvise instead of preparing in advance. Can usually find compelling reasons for whatever they want.	**ENTP** Quick, ingenious, good at many things. Stimulating company, alert, and outspoken. May argue for fun on either side of a question. Resourceful in solving new and challenging problems, but may neglect routine assignments. Apt to turn to one new interest after another. Skillful in finding logical reasons for what they want.
Extraverts	**ESTJ** Practical, realistic, matter-of-fact, with a natural head for business or mechanics. Not interested in abstract theories; want learning to have direct and immediate application. Like to organize and run activities. Often make good administrators; are decisive, quickly move to implement decisions; take care of routine details.	**ESFJ** Warm-hearted, talkative, popular, conscientious, born cooperators, active committee members. Need harmony and may be good at creating it. Always doing something nice for someone. Work best with encouragement and praise. Main interest is in things that directly and visibly affect people's lives.	**ENFJ** Responsive and responsible. Feel real concern for what others think or want, and try to handle things with due regard for the other's feelings. Can present a proposal or lead a group discussion with ease and tact. Sociable, popular, sympathetic. Responsive to praise and criticism. Like to facilitate others and enable people to achieve their potential.	**ENTJ** Frank, decisive. Leaders in activities. Develop and implement comprehensive systems to solve orgnizational problems. Good in anything that requires reasoning and intelligent talk, such as public speaking. Are usualy well informed and enjoy adding to their fund of knowledge.

From Introduction to Type *(5th ed.), Isabel Briggs Myers. Copyright 1993 by Consulting Psychologists Press, Inc. Reproduced with permission.*

■ **TABLE A.2**
Characteristics Frequently Associated with Each Type

Extraversion (E)
- Excellent verbal communicator
- Wide variety of skills and interests
- Strong public speaking skills
- Take initiative
- Networking skills

Sensing (S)
- Extremely resourceful
- Work well with details
- Readily identify and communicate pertinent facts of the problem at hand
- Address and manage the realities of the current situation or problem
- Build morale by appreciating and communicating the positives of the moment

Thinking (T)
- Analytical, logical problem solver
- Objective, reasonable, and fair
- Strong negotiator
- Analyze consequences and implications of difficult decisions
- Identify and see flaws or problems before they happen
- Consistently maintain fair and objective policies and procedures
- Stand firm for principles that are important to the company
- Create and maintain rational, fair systems of operations

Judging (J)
- Organized and methodical
- Coordinate complex projects to successful closure
- Schedule and implement projects, labor hours, and systems
- Recognized for getting tasks done on time and under budget
- Maintain tight controls on operations

Introversion (I)
- Excellent written communicator
- Focused on and attentive to the problems at hand
- Highly skilled and adept within the industry
- Review alternatives thoroughly before making insightful recommendations
- Work quietly and efficiently

Intuition (N)
- Long-term planner
- Recognize unseen business opportunities
- Vision for future possibilities
- Think of new and exciting ideas
- Apply insight to complex problem solving
- Objectively see how seemingly unrelated events and facts tie together
- Anticipate and prepare for future trends within the company and the industry
- Thrive in challenging, ever-changing environments

Feeling (F)
- Work well with a wide variety of people
- Excellent listener
- Create strong bonds with peers, clients, and supervisors
- Excel in a team-oriented environment
- Forecast how others will feel about new issues within the company
- Teach and coach others to be their best
- Stand firm for values that are important to the workforce
- Organize people and tasks harmoniously

Perceiving (P)
- Thrive in fast-paced, competitive environments
- Adapt quickly to ever-changing environments
- Encourage feedback and new ideas from staff
- Review all options thoroughly before making decisions
- Remain flexible and open to the changes common in the workplace

■ **TABLE A.3**
Type Characteristics

Phrases from Combinations of Judgment and External Preferences

Thinking and Judging (TJ)
- Tough-minded, analytical, and instrumental leader
- Make sound decisions based on principles and systems, overall impacts and rational analysis of outcomes

Feeling and Judging (FJ)
- Lead by teaching and inspiring employees
- Observant within corporate culture to create a productive and vibrant work environment

Thinking and Perceiving (TP)
- Objective and critical analysis of operations and excessive expenditures
- Structure a fair and organized system for employees to work within

Feeling and Perceiving (FP)
- Build strong working relationships within teams and various work groups
- Lead and supervise through strong employee support, coaching, and encouragement

---

Phrases from Combinations of Judgment and Perception Preferences

Sensing and Thinking (ST)
- Results- and bottom-line–oriented

Intuition and Thinking (NT)
- Thrive on opportunities for problem solving, analysis, and design

Sensing and Feeling (SF)
- Drawn to opportunities for practical service to people

Intuition and Feeling (NF)
- Recognize and help people reach their full potential

Phrases from Combinations of Direction of Energy and External Orientation

Introversion and Judging (IJ)
- Persevere through challenging tasks and assignments
- Develop organized, well–thought-out systems

Extraversion and Judging (EJ)
- Lead and work quickly and confidently
- Recognized for getting things done

Introversion and Perceiving (IP)
- Extremely flexible within daily operations
- Believe in and work toward sound principles set within the company

Extraversion and Perceiving (EP)
- Thrive in a fast-paced, ever-changing environment
- Readily accept and enjoy new challenges

Adapted from Introduction to Type *(5th ed.), Isabel Briggs Myers. Copyright 1993 by Consulting Psychologists Press. Reprinted with permission.*

■ **TABLE A.4**
Phrases from Combinations of Preferences

Resources

The Art of Speedreading People
*Harness the Power of Personality Type
and Create What You Want in
Business and in Life*
Paul D. Tieger and Barbara Barron-Tieger
Little, Brown and Company, 1998

The Artist's Way
A Spiritual Path to Higher Creativity
Julia Cameron
J. P. Tarcher, 1992

Ask the Master, Book 2
*Surprising Answers That Can Change
Your Life*
Harold Klemp
Eckankar, 1998

Creative Visualization
Shakti Gawain
Bantam Books, 1983

Dare to Win
Jack Canfield and Mark Victor Hansen
Berkley Publishing Group, 1996

Do What You Are
*Discover the Perfect Career for You
Through the Secrets of Personality Type*
Paul D. Tieger and
Barbara Barron-Tieger
Little, Brown and Company, 1995

**Do What You Love, the Money
Will Follow**
Discovering Your Right Livelihood
Marsha Sinetar
Dell Books, 1989

Fusion Leadership
*Unlocking the Subtle Forces That
Change People and Organizations*
Richard L. Daft and Robert H. Lengel
Berrett-Koehler, 1998

Heart & Soul Internet Job Search
*Seven Never-Before-Published Secrets
to Capturing Your Dream Job Using
the Internet*
Chuck Cochran and Donna Peerce
Davies-Black Publishing, 1999

Heart & Soul Resumes
*Seven Never-Before-Published Secrets
to Capturing Heart & Soul in Your
Resume*
Chuck Cochran and Donna Peerce
Davies-Black Publishing, 1998

Heart at Work
*Stories and Strategies for Building
Self-Esteem and Reawakening the
Soul at Work*
Jack Canfield and Jacqueline Miller
McGraw-Hill, 1998

Holy Work
Be Love, Be Blessed, Be a Blessing
Marsha Sinetar
Crossroad Publishing, 1998

How to Master Change in Your Life
*Sixty-Seven Ways to Handle Life's
Toughest Moments*
Mary Carroll Moore
Eckankar, 1997

**How to Stop Worrying
and Start Living**
*Time-Tested Methods for
Conquering Worry*
Dale Carnegie
Pocket Books, 1985

Living, Loving and Learning
Leo F. Buscaglia
Fawcett Books, 1990

Living Your Dreams
Gayle Delaney
HarperSanFrancisco, 1996

Love Is Letting Go of Fear
Gerald G. Jampolsky
Celestial Arts, 1998

Love, Medicine and Miracles
Lessons Learned About Self-Healing
from a Surgeon's Experience with
Exceptional Patients
Bernie S. Siegel
Harperperennial Library, 1990

Love and Survival
The Scientific Basis for the Healing
Power of Intimacy
Dean Ornish
HarperCollins, 1998

Move Ahead with Possibility
Thinking
Robert H. Schuller
Jove Publications, 1986

Out of the Blue
Delight Comes into Our Lives
Mark Victor Hansen and
Barbara Nichols
Harperperennial Library, 1997

Out of Darkness into the Light
A Journey of Inner Healing
Gerald G. Jampolsky
Bantam Doubleday Dell, 1990

Peace, Love and Healing
Bodymind Communication and the Path
to Self-Healing: An Exploration
Bernie S. Siegel
Harperperennial Library, 1990

The Power of Positive Thinking
Norman Vincent Peale
Ballantine Books, 1996

Prescriptions for Living
Inspirational Lessons for a Joyful,
Loving Life
Bernie S. Siegel
HarperCollins, 1998

The Seven Spiritual Laws of Success
Deepak Chopra
Amber-Allen Publishing, 1995

A Spiritual Friendship
Anonymous
Crossroad Publishing, 1999

Success Is a Choice
Ten Steps to Overachieving in Business
and Life
Rick Pitino
Broadway Books, 1997

To Build the Life You Want,
Create the Work You Love
The Spiritual Dimension of
Entrepreneuring
Marsha Sinetar
St. Martin's Griffin, 1996

Way of the Peaceful Warrior
Dan Millman
H. J. Kramer, 1985

What Color Is Your Parachute?
Richard Nelson Bolles
Ten Speed Press, updated annually

What to Say When You Talk
to Your Self
Shad Helmstetter
Pocket Books, 1990

You Can Heal Your Life
Louise L. Hay
Hay House, 1987

You Can't Afford the Luxury
of a Negative Thought
Peter McWilliams
Prelude Press, 1997

About the Authors

CHUCK COCHRAN

Chuck Cochran formally launched the Heart & Soul Career Center in 1991 and has since helped thousands of executives, professionals, and young people with all aspects of their job searches and career development. He cofounded the *Heart & Soul* career book series concept, which implements an insightful and inspirational approach to helping individuals achieve their dreams. With an MBA degree from Vanderbilt University's Owen Graduate School of Management, he has started three successful companies and with this book has coauthored four books on personal and professional development. He is also, with Donna Peerce, a featured career writer for the *Wall Street Journal*'s *National Business Employment Weekly*. He and Donna can be heard regularly on radio and TV talk shows and speak at numerous national and international seminars and workshops.

Chuck knows goals are never achieved by accident and therefore stresses the need for creating a personal mission and objectives that will guide your career and life to wherever you want them to be. As a career counselor, he knows that success in business and the job market depends on one's knowledge, commitment, and focus, and these are the subjects he focuses on. Chuck also works with organizations and businesses in teaching this message, which is key in team building, communication, and organization development. He is an experienced career professional and actively utilizes the *Myers-Briggs Type Indicator* and *Strong Interest Inventory* instruments in his work.

A respected speaker, Chuck has an inspiring and entertaining way of putting his audiences at ease, and he lays a foundation of knowledge and trust that allows the seminar and workshop attendees to openly discuss life and career issues. Participants always walk away with life- and career-changing tools they can implement immediately. Chuck speaks nationally on the topics of success, entrepreneurship, marketing, e-commerce, career development, communication, and organization development.

Recently, Chuck toured Cuba and Hong Kong and studied international business, culture, and their economies. His time at home is spent with his wife, Michelle, and son, Dean. In addition to running his businesses, Chuck continues to write and develop books and programs related to careers and entrepreneurship. Please contact Chuck and/or Donna at their web site that follows.

DONNA PEERCE

Donna Peerce's mission in life is to help people utilize a Heart & Soul approach to finding jobs that they will love and that will fulfill their lifelong dreams. Cofounder of the *Heart & Soul* career book series, Donna has helped thousands of individuals from all over the world find jobs and resolve career issues. She counsels individuals from countries as far away as Singapore and Australia and is dedicated to making a difference and a real impact in people's lives. She is also, with Chuck, a contributing editor and featured career writer for the *Wall Street Journal*'s *National Business Employment Weekly*. Both can be heard regularly on radio and TV talk shows and at numerous national and international seminars and workshops.

Donna began her professional writing career while in elementary school when she published her first short story in a newspaper. This inspired her to continue in her writing endeavors and to combine these with art, broadcast production, and business communications. She has published numerous short stories, essays, greeting cards, and radio and TV commercials, and she has served as a ghostwriter for seven novels and written literally thousands of resumes and business portfolios for career professionals. Throughout her life, she has implemented a Heart & Soul approach to her writing and to her every-day experiences.

While attending Western Kentucky University in Bowling Green, Donna won several literary awards for short stories, essays, and poetry. After graduating with a bachelor of arts degree in radio, television, and journalism, she worked for commercial and public television studios, honing her skills as a producer/director and scriptwriter. Combining her video production skills with writing was a natural for her, and she continues to freelance as a broadcast producer/director and writer. As an international workshop presenter, Donna travels throughout the United States, Canada, and Europe to facilitate creative Heart & Soul writing and career workshops.

With more than twenty years of experience as a professional writer, Donna has worked for international advertising agencies and won prestigious Addy awards for her television commercials.

As an accomplished artist and poet, Donna's work has been published by Blue Mountain Arts, Inc.; Hallmark; American Greetings; and Gibson Greeting Cards. Donna's hobbies include dream study, alternative health study, aerobics, kickboxing, aero-boxing, Pilates, spinning, hiking in the woods, photography, all music, guitar, piano, singing, and travel. While in high school and college, Donna was a member of an all-girl folk rock band and toured parts of the U.S., appearing on state and national TV.

Donna is a world traveler and has roamed the quaint villages of Europe and the ancient islands of Greece in search of her true destiny as well as her ancient past. After numerous years of travel, dream study, and spiritual study, Donna considers herself a "spiritual scientist" and believes that all of life is a spiritual experience and that the real meaning of life and the answers begin within yourself. Her professional goal is to teach people how to put heart and soul into their lives and discover their own inner answers, and to help them find the job of their dreams!

Born on a dairy and tobacco farm in Kentucky, the eldest of eight siblings, Donna is single and resides in Nashville, Tennessee. She began writing resumes in 1988 to supplement her freelance income, and in 1993, joined Chuck at ResumePlus, Inc. Together, they developed the Heart & Soul Career Center, which is now known as one of the most respected and successful career centers in the world. She is currently a member of the National Career Development Association and is on the Group Fitness Committee at the YMCA.

Invitation

Chuck and Donna invite you to write them at the Heart & Soul Career Center, 1808 West End Avenue, Suite 1012, Nashville, TN 37203, or call (615) 329-0300. Or e-mail Donna at dpeerce@mindspring.com and Chuck at heart-soul@mindspring.com. We would love to talk to you about your career and offer ways to help you succeed in reaching for your dreams! We would also like to talk to you if you are interested in career or entrepreneurial opportunities with the Heart & Soul Career Center. What a wonderful thing it is to make a difference in people's lives and make living at it as well!

Visit our web site for additional Heart & Soul books, tool kits, tapes, workshops, and programs.

Heart & Soul Career Center Online:
www.heartsoul.home.mindspring.com

HEART & SOUL TIP

Check out our web site for the latest information on our books, services, and company.

Index

abilities. *See* knowledge, skills, abilities

affirmations: case study example of, 85–86; definition of, 85; negativity and, 85; self-assessment for, 86–87

alignment: benefits of, 7; in career, 2; case study example of, 2–4; common ground for, 4–6; with company. *See* company; knowledge, skills, abilities and, 8–10, 17; obligation regarding, 4; of personal goals, 1–2

anger: case study example of, 81–82; depression and, 83; hiding of, 83; positive uses of, 82–83; power of, 82; trap caused by, 81; types of, 83; walking as method of managing. *See* walking

attitude: arrogant, 52–53; bad, 52; changing of, 67–71; of gratitude, 53–54, 89; during job search, 52–54; negative, 66–71; positive, 66, 68–71, 73, 109; self-assessment of, 67–71; toward others, 67, 72–73

behavior: *Myers-Briggs Type Indicator* instrument for analyzing. *See Myers-Briggs Type Indicator* instrument; and psychological type, 32; trends in, 32, 37; understanding of, 28

beliefs, 80

boss, assessments of, 4–6

career: reinventing yourself during. *See* reinventing, of your self; self-responsibility for, 84–85; stress caused by, 62; wage assessments, 47–48

career map: benefits of, 126; example of, 127; self-assessment of, 128

career mistakes: bad attitude, 52–54; description of, 40; failure to pursue more than one lead at a time, 44–46; incorrect positioning in the marketplace, 46–48; lack of focus or clear sense of purpose, 40–43; little or no follow-up, 55; overstating your qualifications, 59–60; poor interviewing and networking skills, 56–59; poor resume and cover letter, 44; too broad or narrow a scope for your target job, 49–50

career move, 121

career path: broad scope in, 49–50; "easy," 125; narrow scope in, 49–50; selection of, 125

change: case study example of, 75–76; in company, 7–8; creative, 100–102; dreams and, 109, 111–112; effects of, 95; employer versus industry, 117; handling of, 95–96; need for, 113–114; negative thoughts and, 80–81; planned, 96–100; positive thoughts for handling, 109–110; self-assessments and, 104–109; sources of, 116–117; stress and, 75; unplanned, 102–104; viewing of, 75

clique: diversity outside of, 23; formation of, 23

company: assessments of, 7–8, 11–13, 19; case study example of, 19–20; change in, 7–8; culture of, 7–8, 11, 18–19; diversity in, 26–28, 133; knowledge, skills, abilities requirements, 8; personal values and company culture evaluations, 11, 18–19; questions for evaluating, 118–122; strategic goals of, 11–13; SWOT analysis, 11, 14; values of, 118; vision of, 7

cover letter: importance of, 44; writing of, 44

co-workers, diversity of, 22–23, 28–31

creative changes, 100–102

creativity, 100

criticism: acceptance of, 74; benefits of, 74; stress reduction and, 74

culture: of company, 7–8, 11, 18–19; elements of, 7

depression: anger and, 83; emotional, 83

diversity: benefits of, 32; case study example of, 26–28; in company, 26–28, 133; embracing of, 22–23, 28–31, 37; in friendships, 23–25; handling of, 130; importance of, 6; strength from, 22–23; valuing of, 22–23, 32

dreams, 109, 111–112

education: financial considerations, 124–125; formal, 123–125; informal, 124–126

emotional depression, 83

employer: assessments of, 7–8, 11–13, 19, 117–118; case study example of, 19–20; changes in, 7–8, 117–118; culture of, 7–8, 11, 18–19; job search research regarding, 50–52; knowledge, skills, abilities requirements, 8; personal values and company culture evaluations, 11, 18–19; questions for evaluating, 118–122; researching of, 49–51; strategic goals of, 11–13; SWOT analysis, 11, 14; vision of, 7

experiences: diversity of, 22; effects of, 21–22

failure, 65, 96–97

feelings, avoidance of, 83

follow-up, after sending resume, 55

formal education, 123–125

friends: assessment of, 23–25; cliques, 23; diversity seeking in, 23–25; victim role and, 85

goals: alignment of, 1–2; of company, 11–13; failure to achieve, 96–97; planned changes and, 96–100; self-assessment of, 11, 15–17, 108, 121; setting of, 96–100

gratitude: attitude of, 53–54, 89; effects of, 89

income expectations: assessments of, 46, 48; case study example of, 47; job search and, 46; methods for determining, 47–48; underestimating of, 46–47

industry: assessments of, 118–120; versus employer, 117

informal education, 124–126

internal dialogue, 93

interviewing: case study example of, 56; improvement in, 56; questions commonly asked, 56–58